Principals of Civil Procedure

Law School Notes
2018

FitchLaw, Inc.

Copyright:
Copyright 2018 FitchLaw. All rights reserved. No part of this publication may be stored in a retrieval system, transmitted, or reproduced in any way, including but not limited to photocopy, photographs, magnetic, or other record, without the prior agreement and written permission of the publisher.

The author and publisher have made their best efforts to prepare this book. The author and publisher make no representation or warranties of any kind with regards to the completeness or accuracy of the contents herein and accepts no liability of any kind, including but not limited to performance, merchantability, fitness for any particular purpose or any losses or damages of any kind caused or alleged to be caused directly or indirectly from this book.

Trademarks:
FitchLaw Inc., has attempted throughout this book to distinguish proprietary trademarks from descriptive terms by following the capitalization style used by the manufacturer.

Published by: FitchLaw Inc.

FitchLaw Inc., welcome corrections and comments on its documents. In addition to comments, please send comments on typographical, formatting, or other errors. Simply make a copy of the relevant page, mark the error, and send it to fitchlawupdates@gmail.com.

Books and testing materials are available at special quantity discounts to use as premiums and sales promotions, or for corporate training programs, as well as other educational programs.

Printed in the United States of America. No part of this work may be reproduced or transmitted in any form or by any means, electronic, manual, photocopying, recording, or by any information storage and retrieval systems, without prior written permission of the publisher.

ISBN-13: 978-1986181853 (paperback)

Contents

1 Overview — 5
- 1.1 Introduction — 5
- 1.2 Jurisdiction — 5
- 1.3 Governing law — 8
- 1.4 Pleading — 9
- 1.5 Joinder, Counterclaims, Crossclaims, Impleader — 10
- 1.6 Discovery — 12
- 1.7 Summary judgment — 13
- 1.8 Jury trials — 13
- 1.9 Appeals — 13
- 1.10 Preclusion — 14

2 Structure of a Lawsuit — 16
- 2.1 Preliminaries — 16
- 2.2 Which Court? — 16
- 2.3 Complaint, Filing, and Service of Process — 16
- 2.4 Responding to the Complaint — 16
- 2.5 Discovery, Summary Judgment, Settlement — 17
- 2.6 Trial — 17
- 2.7 Post-Trial or Post-Judgment Motions — 18
- 2.8 Appeal — 18

3 Provisional Remedies — 19
- 3.1 Statute of Limitations: *United States v. Kubrick* — 19
- 3.2 Due Process Requirements — 19
- 3.3 Remedies — 19
- 3.4 Notice and Opportunity to be Heard: *Fuentes v. Shevin* — 20
- 3.5 Deprivation and Due Process: *Connecticut v. Doehr* — 21

4 Jurisdiction — 22
- 4.1 Personal Jurisdiction — 22
    - 4.1.1 Territorial Power: *Pennoyer v. Neff* — 23
    - 4.1.2 Jurisdiction Over Out-of-State Drivers: *Hess v. Pawloski* — 24
    - 4.1.3 Minimum Contacts: *International Shoe Co. v. Washington* — 25
    - 4.1.4 Purposeful Availment: *World-Wide Volkswagen Corp. v. Woodson* — 25
    - 4.1.5 Purposeful Availment II: *Burger King Corp. v. Rudzewicz* — 27
    - 4.1.6 Defenses to Personal Jurisdiction — 28
    - 4.1.7 General and Specific Jurisdiction: *Goodyear Dunlop Tires Operations, S.A. v. Brown* — 28
    - 4.1.8 Product Distribution and Purposeful Direction: *J. McIntyre Machinery, Ltd. v. Nicastro* — 29
    - 4.1.9 Long-Arm Statutes — 29

	4.1.10	Online Activity and Long-Arm Statutes: *Bensusan Rest. Corp v. King*	30
	4.1.11	FRCP 4(k): Territorial Limits of Effective Service	31
	4.1.12	Challenging the *Pennoyer* Framework for Quasi In Rem Actions: *Shaffer v. Heitner*	31
	4.1.13	Physical Presence and Personal Jurisdiction: *Burnham v. Superior Court of Cal.*	32
	4.1.14	"Notice Reasonably Calculated" *Mullane v. Central Hanover Bank & Trust*	34
	4.1.15	Service by Mail: *Jones v. Flowers*	35
	4.1.16	Contractual Consent to Jurisdiction: *Carnival Cruise Lines, Inc. v. Shrute*	35
4.2	Subject Matter Jurisdiction and Venue		37
	4.2.1	Federal Question Jurisdiction	38
		4.2.1.1 Well Pleaded Complaint: *Louisville & Nashville R.R. Co. v. Mottley*	39
		4.2.1.2 The Kaleidoscope and the Welcome Mat: *Grable & Sons Metal Prods. v. Darue Eng. & Manuf.*	39
	4.2.2	Diversity Jurisdiction	41
		4.2.2.1 Complete Diversity: *Mas v. Perry*	41
		4.2.2.2 The Corporate Nerve Center: *Hertz Corp. v. Friend*	42
4.3	Supplemental Jurisdiction		43
		4.3.0.3 Common Nucleus of Operative Fact: *United Mine Workers of Am. v. Gibbs*	43
		4.3.0.4 Supplemental Jurisdiction and Third-Party Defendants: *Owen Equip. & Erection Co. v. Kroger*	44
4.4	Removal		45
		4.4.0.5 Removal and Subject Matter Jurisdiction: *Caterpillar Inc. v. Williams*	45
4.5	Venue, Transfer, and *Forum Non Conveniens*		46
	4.5.1	*Forum Non Conveniens* and Differences in Substantive Law: *Piper Aircraft Co. v. Reyno*	46

5 The Governing Law in the Federal Courts — 48
- 5.1 General Law over State Law: *Swift v. Tyson* — 48
- 5.2 No Federal General Common Law: *Erie R.R. Co. v. Tompkins* — 49
- 5.3 "Outcome Determinative" Test: *Guaranty Trust v. York* — 51
- 5.4 Really Regulating Procedure: *Sibbach v. Wilson & Co.* — 53
- 5.5 "Byrd Balancing": *Byrd v. Blue Ridge Rural Elec. Coop.* — 53
- 5.6 State vs. Federal Procedural Rules: *Hanna v. Plumer* — 54
- 5.7 Applying the *Hanna* Test: *Walker v. Armco Steel Corp.* — 55
- 5.8 Standards of Appellate Review: *Gasperini v. Center for Humanities* — 56
- 5.9 Federal Common Law: *Clearfield Trust Co v. United States* — 56

6 Pleading — 58
- 6.1 FRCP 8: General Rules of Pleading — 59
- 6.2 FRCP 10: Form of Pleadings — 60
- 6.3 Liberal Pleading Requirements: *Swierkiewicz v. Sorema, N.A.* — 60
- 6.4 Plausible Pleadings: *Bell Atlantic v. Twombly* — 60
- 6.5 Affirming *Twombly*: *Ashcroft v. Iqbal* — 61
- 6.6 Pleading in the Alternative: *McCormick v. Kopmann* — 61
- 6.7 Sanctions: *Zuk v. E. Penn. Psychiatric Institute* — 62
- 6.8 FRCP 11: Signing, Representations, Sanctions — 62
- 6.9 FRCP 12: Defenses and Objections — 63
- 6.10 Explicit Affirmation or Denial: *Zielinski v. Philadelphia Piers* — 63
- 6.11 FRCP 15: Amended and Supplemental Pleadings — 64
- 6.12 Amendments Relating Back: *Worthington v. Wilson* — 65

7 Joinder, Counterclaims, and Crossclaims — 66
- 7.1 FRCP 18: Joinder of Claims — 68
- 7.2 FRCP 42: Consolidation; Separate Trials — 68
- 7.3 FRCP 13: Counterclaim and Crossclaim — 68
- 7.4 Counterclaims and Supplemental Jurisdiction: *Jones v. Ford Motor Credit Co.* — 68
- 7.5 Jurisdiction over Crossclaims: *Fairview Park v. Al Monzo* — 69
- 7.6 Parties and Standing — 70
- 7.7 Series of Transactions or Occurrences: *Kedra v. City of Philadelphia* — 70
- 7.8 Permissive and Necessary Parties: *Temple v. Synthes Corp.* — 70
- 7.9 Necessary vs. Indispensable Parties: *Helzberg's Diamond Shops v. Valley West Des Moines Shopping Center* — 71
- 7.10 FRCP 14(a)–(b): Third-Party Practice — 71
- 7.11 *Banks v. City of Emeryville* — 72
- 7.12 FRCP 24: Intervention — 72

8 Discovery — 73
- 8.1 FRCP 26: Duty to Disclose; General Provisions Governing Discovery — 74
- 8.2 FRCP 29: Stipulations about Discovery Procedure — 75
- 8.3 FRCP 30: Depositions by Oral Examination — 75
- 8.4 FRCP 33–36 — 75
- 8.5 Privileges and Sanctions — 76
  - 8.5.1 Work Product Privilege: *Hickman v. Taylor* — 76
  - 8.5.2 Work-Product Doctrine — 78
  - 8.5.3 FRCP 37: Failure to Make Disclosures or to Cooperate in Discovery; Sanctions — 78

9 Summary Judgment — 79
- 9.1 FRCP 56 — 80
- 9.2 Summary Judgment: *Adickes v. S.H. Kress & Co.* — 80
- 9.3 *Celotex Corp. v. Catrett* — 81
- 9.4 *Arnstein v. Porter* — 82
- 9.5 Disagreement about the Existence of a Dispute of Material Fact: *Scott v. Harris* — 82

10 Jury Trials — 84
- 10.1 Overview and Background — 84
- 10.2 Judgment as a Matter of Law: *Simblest v. Maynard* — 85
- 10.3 Reasonable Inference of Negligence: *Sioux City & Pac R.R. Co. v. Stout* — 86
- 10.4 FRCP 50: Judgment as a Matter of Law in a Jury Trial; Related Motion for a New Trial; Conditional Ruling — 87
- 10.5 FRCP 59: New Trial; Altering or Amending a Judgment — 87
- 10.6 Overview of Post-Trial Motions — 87
- 10.7 Sacredness of Juries: *Tanner v. United States* — 88
- 10.8 New Trials: *Spurlin v. Gen. Motors* — 89

11 Appeals — 90
- 11.1 Collateral Order Doctrine: *Digital Equip. Corp. v. Desktop Direct* — 91
- 11.2 28 U.S.C. § 1257: Supreme Court Review of State Court Decisions — 91
- 11.3 28 U.S.C. § 1291: Federal Appellate Court Jurisdiction — 92
- 11.4 28 U.S.C. § 1292: Federal Interlocutory Appeals — 92

12 Preclusion — 93
- 12.1 Consequences of Final Judgment: *Federated Department Stores, Inc. v. Moitie* — 94
- 12.2 Claim Preclusion: *Davis v. DART* — 96
- 12.3 Claim Splitting: *Staats v. County of Sawyer* — 96
- 12.4 Collateral Estoppel: *Levy v. Kosher Overseers Ass'n of Am.* — 97
- 12.5 Informal Proceedings and Issue Preclusion: *Jacobs v. CBS* — 98
- 12.6 Virtual Representation: *Taylor v. Sturgell* — 98
  - 12.6.1 Preclusion Against Other Parties: *Parklane Hosiery v. Shore* — 99

13 Class Actions — 101
- 13.1 FRCP 23: Class Actions — 101
- 13.2 *Chandler v. Southwest Jeep-Eagle, Inc.* — 102
- 13.3 *Wal Mart Stores, Inc. v. Dukes* — 102

§ 1 Overview

1.1 Introduction

1. Themes throughout the class:

    (a) Procedure as **policy**: how does procedure express values about justice?

    (b) Procedure as **strategy**: how do actors use process strategically?

    (c) Procedure and **power**: whom do rules benefit? Does access to rulemakers matter? Why have rules at all? How do state vs. federal issues come into play?

2. Goals of the FRCP: **just, speedy, and inexpensive** determination.

3. You can't sleep on your rights. *Kubrick*.

4. **Due process analysis**: was there deprivation? Was there **notice and opportunity to be heard**? *Fuentes*. Usually a hearing is needed before deprivation, and balance the parties' interests. *Doehr*.

1.2 Jurisdiction

1. **Personal jurisdiction**.

    (a) Territorial power framework—outdated. *Pennoyer*.

    (b) New test: "**minimum contacts** consistent with traditional notions of fair play and substantial justice." *International Shoe*.

    (c) **General jurisdiction**: defendant has substantial enough contacts with the state such that any dispute can be litigated there. *Goodyear* (foreign-manufactured tires caused deaths of Americans).

    (d) **Specific jurisdiction**: PJ is based on contacts related to the specific dispute.

    (e) **Purposeful availment**: benefiting from the state's laws. Factors: state's interest in adjudicating the dispute, plaintiff's interest in convenient and effective relief, interstate judicial system's interest in efficient resolution, and states' shared interest in substantive social policy.[1] *World-Wide Volkswagen* (car blowing up in Oklahoma).

    (f) **Purposeful direction**: intending to sell products in the forum state. *J. McIntyre* (tort claim against British manufacturer).

    (g) **Long-arm statutes**: authorize courts within constitutional limits to exercise jurisdiction over people outside their borders. *Bensusan* (restaurant website).

---

[1] Casebook p. 191.

- (h) **Rule 4(k)**: PJ analysis in federal courts.
    - i. If the claim arises under *state* law, apply the state long-arm statute.
    - ii. Under **federal** law: is there a federal long-arm statute? If so, apply it and check whether the defendant has minimum contacts with the US. (If there is no personal jurisdiction in any state, you can sue in any district court.) If not, apply the state long-arm statute.
- (i) **Physical presence** establishes PJ. *Burnham* (divorce dispute). **Property presence** does not. *Shaffer* (shares of Greyhound).
- (j) There is instability in stream-of-commerce cases. *J. McIntyre.*
- (k) Plaintiff must take adequate steps to ensure **notice and opportunity to be heard**—"notice reasonably calculated, under all the circumstances, to apprise interested parties of the pendency of the action and afford them an opportunity to present their objections." *Mullane* (judicial settlement of a common trust fund).
- (l) **Forum selection clauses** are enforceable in contract of adhesion. *Carnival Cruise Lines.*

2. **Subject matter jurisdiction.**
    - (a) Sources: Article III, federal jurisdictional statutes, state long-arm statutes.
    - (b) **Cannot be waived** for structural reasons. Parties and courts can raise SMJ issues at any time, as SCOTUS did *sua sponte* in *Mottley* (railroad pass contract dispute).
    - (c) **Federal question jurisdiction.**
        - i. Authorized under Article III and 28 U.S.C. § 1331.
        - ii. Any federal "ingredient" is sufficient.
        - iii. Even if there is no federal cause of action, FQSMJ is available in cases that **"implicate significant federal issues"**. *Grable* (IRS property seizure; "kaleidoscope" and "welcome mat").
        - iv. The **well pleaded complaint rule**: an anticipated federal defense does not establish FQSMJ. *Mottley* (railroad pass contract dispute).
    - (d) **Diversity jurisdiction.**
        - i. Article III and 28 U.S.C. § 1332.
        - ii. DSMJ exists when parties are from diverse states and the **amount in controversy** is above $75,000.
        - iii. **Complete diversity**: no plaintiff can be from the same state as any defendant. *Mas* (peeping landlord).

iv. **Corporations** are citizens of their **state of incorporation** and where their **"nerve center"** is located. *Hertz* (class action in California).

(e) **Supplemental jurisdiction**.

i. A claim without jurisdiction can **ride the coattails** of a claim *with* valid jurisdiction.

ii. 28 U.S.C. § 1367.

iii. Analysis:
- Is there a claim with valid jurisdiction?
- Do the supplemental claims arise from **same case or controversy**? § 1367(a) and **Gibbs** (mining contracts—"common nucleus of operative fact").
- Is the original claim based on diversity? If yes, there is no supplemental jurisdiction for claims *by plaintiffs* against third-party defendants if the claim would destroy complete diversity. Goal is to disallow jurisdiction over defendants that would otherwise be unavailable. § 1367(b) and *Kroger* (crane, electrocution).
- Courts are not required to grant supplemental jurisdiction. § 1367(c).

(f) **Removal**.

i. State → to federal. 28 U.S.C. § 1441 (allowing removal) and 1446 (procedure).

ii. Removal confers venue on the district court. 1390(c).

iii. Unavailable in diversity cases where a defendant is a citizen of the state.

iv. Only defendants can remove and all defendants must consent.

v. Removal does not expand SMJ. *Caterpillar* (employment contracts; no SMJ for private contract disputes).

vi. Plaintiff is **master of the complaint** and free to bring action in state *or* federal court.

(g) **Venue**.

i. Which district can you sue in? 28 U.S.C. § 1390 (scope), 1391 (venue generally), 1404 (transfer—apply law of original venue), 1406 (dealing with improper venue—apply law of new venue). Courts can dismiss *or* transfer.

ii. Waivable.

iii. Transfer is available between districts.

(h) *Forum non conveniens*.

i. Is there a more convenient forum where the case should be adjudicated?

ii. Standard: casebook p. 474.
iii. Differences in substantive law are insufficient for FNC unless the law in the target forum is egregiously bad.
iv. Successful FNC motions result in dismissal. *Piper* (plane crash in Scotland).

1.3 Governing law

1. **General federal common law**: "The common law is not a **brooding omnipresence** in the sky, but the articulate voice of some sovereign or quasi sovereign that can be identified . . . "—Holmes.

2. *Swift*: RDA (28 U.S.C. § 1652) means federal courts should apply **federal** substantive common law.

3. *Erie*: RDA means federal courts should apply **state** substantive common law. No more federal general common law.

4. REA (28 U.S.C. §§ 2071–77) authorizes FRCP—"shall not abridge, enlarge, or modify any substantive right" (2072).

5. **Outcome determinative test**: if choice of law would significantly affect the outcome, apply state substantive law. *York* (statute of limitations in a fraud case).

6. *Byrd* **balancing**: strong federal interests can weigh in favor of applying state law. *Byrd* (employment status of a worker injured while connecting power lines).

7. A rule is procedural if it **really regulates procedure**. It can be substantial without being substantive. *Sibbach* (compulsory medical exam).

8. *Hanna* **tests**: when to apply federal procedural rules.

    (a) What is the source of the procedural rule?

    i. Congressional rule, i.e., FRCP or statute ("*Hanna* holding"):
    - Is the federal rule **pertinent**? I.e., is there an unavoidable conflict with a state procedural rule? If no, apply the federal rule. If yes:
    - Is the federal rule **valid**?[2]
        – Is it **constitutional**? I.e., is it "rationally capable of classification as procedural?"
        – Is it consistent with the **Rules Enabling Act**? I.e., does it "really regulate procedure" (*Sibbach*) without abridging substantive rights?

---

[2]No FRCP has ever been found to be invalid, thought the Court has interpreted them narrowly to preserve their validity.

- → If the rule is invalid, apply the state rule. Otherwise, apply the federal rule. (To hold otherwise would "disembowel" Article III or the REA. Casebook p. 523.)

  i. Judge-made rule ("*Hanna* dictum"):
     - Is the difference between the state and federal rules **outcome determinative**? If not, apply the federal rule. If yes:
     - Does the difference implicate the twin aims of *Erie?*
       A. Does the difference encourage **forum shopping**?
       B. Does the difference cause **inequitable administration of the law**. Can you explain to your client why being in federal vs. state court makes a difference?
       C. If the difference *does* implicate both the twin aims, apply the state rule. Otherwise, apply the federal rule.

9. Federal substantive common law still applies under rare circumstances. *Clearfield Trust* (stolen WPA paycheck).

1.4 Pleading

1. Four parts (FRCP 8 and 10):

   (a) **Parties**: who are we?

   (b) **PJ, SMJ, Venue**: how are we here?

   (c) **Subject of the case**: why are we here?

   (d) **Remedy sought**: what do we want?

2. **Defenses** (12):

   - (b) Defenses by motion. Must be made before responsive pleading.
   - (g) Motions can be joined. The following are **waived** if not brought with the first response to the complaint (motion or pleading): (2) PJ, (3) venue, (4) insufficient process, (5) insufficient service of process.
   - (h)(2) 12(b)(6), compulsory joinder, and defenses are **not waived** and can be raised in pleadings, in 12(c) motions, or at trial (but they cannot be raised in a second pre-answer motion).
   - h(3) SMJ can be raised at any time, even if omitted in first pleading.
   - 12(b)(6) can be raised **at any time** during trial. 12(h)(2).

3. Can amend within 21 days or with permission. 15.

4. Can amend *once* in response to 12(b), (e), (f). 15(a)(1)(B).

5. **Motion to dismiss for failure to state a claim** (12)(b)(6):

   (a) Defendant makes the motion.

(b) Accept the plaintiff's allegations as true.

(c) View the evidence in the light most favorable to the plaintiff.

(d) Deny unless "clear that no relief could be granted under any set of facts that could be proved consistent with the complaint." *Swierkiewicz*.

(e) Liberal policy of leave to amend in response to a 12(b)(6) motion.

6. Original pleading requirements were liberal: **"short and plain statement"**. 8(a).

7. *Conley*: do not grant 12(b)(6) "unless it appears beyond doubt that the plaintiff can prove no set of facts in support of his claim which would entitle him to relief."

8. *Swierkiewicz*: only need to plead a legally cognizable claim. No need to produce evidence.

9. *Twombly*: a pleading must be not merely *conceivable* but *plausible*.

    (a) Pleading must contain a short and plain statement (Rule 8).

    (b) The court accepts facts as true.

    (c) The court draws all reasonable inferences and resolves all ambiguities in favor of the plaintiff.

    (d) The court determines whether the complain is *plausible on its face*, meaning it must be more than a mere possibility and not merely consistent with the defendant's liability.

    (e) Plaintiffs must "nudge[] their claims across the line from conceivable to plausible."

    (f) E.g., in *Twombly*, the district court granted the defendants' 12(b)(6) motion. 2nd Cir. reversed, holding that ILECs failed to show that there is "no set of facts that would support P's claim." SCOTUS reversed, granting the motion.

10. **Pleading in the alternative**: can plead multiple inconsistent claims—spaghetti on the wall. *McCormick* (drunk driving death).

11. **Rule 11** covers attorney duties and sanctions. *Zuk* (sanctions for legally and factually inadequate claims in a university copyright dispute).

12. **Responsive pleadings** must explicitly affirm or deny each element of a claim. *Zielinksi* (forklift jousting).

1.5 Joinder, Counterclaims, Crossclaims, Impleader

1. Each claim requires supp. J or independent SMJ.

2. Supp. J always applies except in diversity cases with specific circumstances. § 1367, *Gibbs*, *Kroger*.

1 OVERVIEW

3. **Joinder of claims** (18(a)): any pleader can join claims. Each requires supp. J.

4. **Joinder of parties**:

   (a) **Permissive** (20): (a)(1) **multiple plaintiffs** (same T&O and common Q), (a)(2) plaintiff can name **multiple co-defendants** (same requirements). Each party must meet jurisdiction requirements. D's can pool claims to meet amount in controversy.

   (b) **Compulsory** (19) when:

   i. there can be no relief (19(a)(1)(A)), or

   ii. it would prejudice the absentee (19(a)(1)(B)(i)), or

   iii. it would cause one of the current parties to be exposed to multiple or inconsistent obligations (but not necessarily inconsistent *judgments*) (19(a)(1)(B)(ii)).

   (c) If an SMJ or PJ problem prevents joinder, court can decide to proceed or dismiss. 19(b) and *Helzberg* (jewelry store lease).

5. Two types of **counterclaims**:

   (a) **Compulsory**: same T&O. Forfeited if not raised. 13(a), *Jones v. Ford* (racial discrimination and car loans).

   (b) **Permissive**: any non-compulsory counterclaim. It can be completely unrelated but requires independent supp. J. *May be* within supp. J if it has a "loose factual connection" to the T&O. 13(b), *Jones v. Ford*. *Compulsory* counterclaims, by contrast, have a "logical relationship" to the original controversy. *Jones*.

6. A **third-party defendant** can counterclaim against the original defendant or the original plaintiff. 14(a).

7. **Crossclaims** are claims between co-defendants or co-plaintiffs. Same T&O. 13(g).

8. **Impleader** (14(a) and *Banks*):

   (a) Can implead for liability to plaintiff, but not for independent claims.

   (b) Can't be used to suggest different defendants.

   (c) Can join a claim in addition to the impleaded claim.

   (d) Requires PJ.

   (e) Supplemental jurisdiction applies if same T&O.

   (f) Third-party defendants can assert **claims of their own** (and supplemental jurisdiction will apply), including:

   i. Counterclaims against the third-party plaintiff.

   ii. Crossclaims against other third-party defendants.

iii. Counterclaims against the primary plaintiff if (a) same T&O or (b) if the primary plaintiff asserted a claim directly against the third-party defendant.

iv. Impleader claims against others not already in the suit.

9. **Intervention** (24):

    (a) Intervention requires independent SMJ.

    (b) **Intervention of right** (24(a)):

    i. "claims an interest relating to the **property or transaction**" at issue;

    ii. disposing of the action would "impair or impede the movant's ability to protect its interest"; and

    iii. the interest is not adequately represented by the existing parties.

    (c) **Permissive** (24(b)): Can intervene with a claim or defense with a common Q. Court had discretion.

10. **Supp. J** over counterclaims: for *compulsory* claims, yes (because they arise from the same T&O); for *permissive* claims, probably not (because they are unrelated), but maybe if there is a "loose factual connection" (*Jones v. Ford*).

1.6 Discovery

1. Generally broad and flexible, like the pleading and joinder rules. Scope: 26(b).

2. Interrogatories, requests for production/inspection, depositions.

3. Process: informal investigation, discovery plan (26(f)), initial mandatory disclosures (26(a)(1)(A)), protective orders (26(c)), depositions (27, 28, 30–32), interrogatories (33), production (34).

4. Evidence is relevant if "(a) it has any tendency to make a fact more or less probable than it would be without the evidence; and (b) the fact is of consequence in determining the action." F.R.Evid. 401.

5. Privileges/work product (26(b)(3) and *Hickman* [sunk tugboat]).

6. Physical/mental exams (35).

7. Requests for admission (36).

8. Motions to compel/sanctions (37).

1.7 Summary judgment

1. **Failure to state a claim** (12(b)(6)): tests the sufficiency of *only* the allegations (no facts). Assuming they're true, is there a valid claim? **Discovery-worthy?** Evaluation criteria: see pleading § 1.4.4 above. If any evidence is involved, it becomes an SJ motion.

2. **Motion for summary judgment** (56): Any party can raise on any claim or defense. Tests factual allegations and legal contentions. Granted if "there is not genuine dispute as to any material fact and the movant is entitled to judgment as a matter of law." **Trial-worthy?**

    (a) Based on **affidavits** and **discovery materials**. Both parties must "properly support" their assertions. 56(e).

    (b) Movant bears the burden of persuasion.

    (c) *Adickes*: D's motion for SJ denied conspiracy but failed to show that there were no policemen present, which permitted the inference that there *was* a conspiracy. Although Adickes did not respond with admissible materials, D failed to make its prima facie case in its motion, so no SJ for D.

    (d) *Celotex*: movant can show that there is no evidence that the other side will be able to prove its case. P could not show that D's product caused the injuries, so summary judgment was proper. (Now, the FRCP require movant to **explain in detail** why an element is missing—56(c)(1)(A)).

    (e) Must be more than "metaphysical uncertainty." *Scott v. Harris*.

    (f) Runs the risk of becoming a form of discovery because "intimations of mortality" can lead the parties to muster their strongest possible arguments.

    (g) Granted if there is "but one conclusion that reasonable men could have reached." *Simblest*.

1.8 Jury trials

1. **JMOL/Renewed JMOL** (50): a reasonable jury could not find for one party based on the evidence. **Jury-worthy?**

2. **New trial** (59): (1) procedural errors or (2) against **"great weight"**. *Spurlin* (bus brake failure; evidence was "at best conflicting").

1.9 Appeals

1. **Final judgment rule** (state § 1257, federal § 1291, interlocutory § 1292) and **collateral order exception** (*Digital*, appealing from a decision it viewed as final).

2. Any dismissal is final except for jurisdiction, venue, or rule 19. 41(b).

3. Appellant must have **preserved the issue**.

4. 3 standards of review:

    (a) **Clear error/abuse of discretion**: reviewing the judge's factual determinations—e.g., new trial, bench trials. 52(a)(6).

    (b) **De novo**: pure question of law, e.g. JMOL, SJ, 12(b)(6).

    (c) **Complete absence of proof**: reviewing the jury's verdict—rare.

1.10 Preclusion

1. **Claim preclusion**: the same plaintiff cannot relitigate a *claim* after it's been decided. Meant to encourage P to bring all claims in A1. Same rationale for compulsory counterclaims.

    (a) Same parties.

    (b) Final judgment on the merits (yes: judgment after trial affirmed on appeal; no: PJ, SMJ, venue; gray area: 12(b)(6), SJ, failure to prosecute, dismissal under sanction—which count as adjudications on the merits in federal court [41(b)]).

    (c) Same cause of action as A1 (same transaction or occurrence).

    (d) Narrow exceptions: agreement/statute, egregious judgment in A1, lack of jurisdiction over A1 (*Staats*).

    Issue preclusion: cannot relitigate an *issue* after it's been decided.

    (a) Same issue.

    (b) Actually litigated and decided.

    (c) Full and fair opportunity to litigate.

    (d) Necessary to the judgment.

    (e) Applies **only to parties in the original suit** (*Taylor*).

2. **Defensive non-mutual collateral estoppel**: shield. A defendant can prevent a plaintiff from relitigating a claim that he had previously asserted and lost against another defendant. *Blonder-Tongue* (patentee whose patent was found invalid cannot relitigate the validity of the patent against another defendant). Gives plaintiffs the incentive to join all potential defendants in the first action.

3. **Offensive non-mutual collateral estoppel**: sword. A plaintiff seeks to prevent a defendant from relitigating an issue the defendant had lost in an earlier trial. May be unfair because the defendant may not have had an incentive to vigorously litigate the issue in the earlier case. It encourages a "wait-and-see" strategy on plaintiffs' part. The court has discretion

to disallow preclusion if (1) the plaintiff could have easily joined A1 and (2) it's not somehow unfair to the defendant. *Parklane* (Parklane cannot relitigate issues about a merger because it had already lost on those issues against the SEC).

§ 2 Structure of a Lawsuit

2.1 Preliminaries

1. Find a lawyer.

2. Learn the facts.

3. Determine the dispute and remedy.

2.2 Which Court?

1. *Personal jurisdiction*: there must be a minimal level of contact between the defendant and the court's territorial sovereign (e.g., the state).

2. *Subject matter jurisdiction*: federal courts have higher thresholds than state courts. (e.g., interstate disputes in amounts above $75,000). In cases of overlap, plaintiff can choose.

3. *Venue*: usually must have some connection to the place where the dispute occurred.

2.3 Complaint, Filing, and Service of Process

1. *Complaint*: plaintiff's statement of claims. Sometimes called petition or declaration.

2. *Filing*: plaintiff files a complaint at the courthouse. This is when the suit commences.

3. *Summons*: served to each defendant.

2.4 Responding to the Complaint

1. Preliminary objections:

    (a) Disputes over territory or venue.

    (b) Motions (to dismiss or quash).

    (c) *Memorandum of law*: the legal arguments supporting a request.

2. *Default judgment*: occurs if the defendant does nothing. Can be set aside if justified.

3. Pleading in response to the complaint:

    (a) In complaints, defendant don't try to prove their case–only to assert what he hopes can be proved.

    (b) *Cause of action*: the violation of law in question.

2 STRUCTURE OF A LAWSUIT

   (c) *General demurrer*: "even if you're right, you're not entitled to recover anything." I.e., so what?

   (d) By default, defendants are deemed to admit allegations they don't deny.

4. Defendant's answer:

   (a) *Negative defenses*: contesting the facts.

   (b) *Affirmative defenses*: contending other factual circumstances.

   (c) *Motion to strike*: e.g., if plaintiff thinks defendant's answer is insufficient in points of substantive law.

5. Some jurisidictions allow the plaintiff to make a reply to the defendant's answer; otherwise, the answer is deemed denied by default.

2.5 Discovery, Summary Judgment, Settlement

1. *Discovery*: each side investigates its opponent's claims.

2. *Interrogatories*: written questions.

3. *Request for production*: documents, opportunities to inspect, other relevant items.

4. *Depositions*: Party questions a witness on camera and/or before a court reporter.

5. *Summary judgment*: Can be granted if something crucial can be determined beyond legitimate dispute.

6. *Affidavit*: Sworn statement.

7. *Pretrial conference*: attempt to resolve the dispute before litigating.

2.6 Trial

1. *At law*: for damages; can be tried by a jury.

2. *In equity*: e.g., for an injunction; normally triable without jury.

3. Jury selection: voir dire, challenge for cause, limited number of peremptory challenges.

4. Trial process:

   (a) Opening statements.

   (b) Case in chief (plaintiff).

   (c) Direct and cross examination of witnesses.

   (d) Plaintiff rests.

- (e) Defendants can request judgment as a matter of law if they believe the claim is invalid.
- (f) Case in chief (defendant).
- (g) Adverse witness: plaintiff himself is called.
- (h) Either side can again call for a judgment as a matter of law.
- (i) Closing argument (plaintiff).
- (j) Closing argument (defendant).
- (k) Judge instructs jury; jury deliberates and returns verdict.
- (l) Jury often (but not always) must be unanimous.

2.7 Post-Trial or Post-Judgment Motions

1. Judgment *non obstante veredicto* (j.n.o.v.): judgment notwithstanding the verdict, e.g., in response to earlier motions for judgment as a matter of law.
2. Parties can seek a new trial on the basis of procedural errors.

2.8 Appeal

1. Can only happen after final judgment, even if there's a gross error early in the process.
2. *Interlocutory appeal*: in some jurisdictions, appeal can be made before final judgment.
3. *Mandamus*: requires the judge to do something.
4. *Prohibition*: on the judge; usually comes from an appellate court in the form of a writ of prohibition.
5. *Reversible error*: something on which an appellate court can reverse a decision and call a new trial.
6. *Harmless error*: didn't affect the outcome of the trial.
7. Appellate review is almost always on the basis of law, not on fact, unless there is "no substantial evidence" to support a factual determination.
8. Appellate court will usually only consider objections that were raised in the trial court.

§ 3 Provisional Remedies

3.1 Statute of Limitations: *United States v. Kubrick*

The statute of limitations tolls when the plaintiff becomes aware of the existence and cause of his injury, not when he becomes aware of malpractice.

1. Kubrick was rendered partially deaf from neomycin treatment at a Veterans Administration hospital. He discovered the possibility of malpractice only after the two year statute of limitations had expired.

2. The precise issue was whether the claim accrues when the plaintiff is aware of the existence and cause of his injury or when he is also aware of the possibility of malpractice.

3. Justice White: there's a clear rule here. The statute of limitations tolls when the plaintiff becomes aware of the existence and cause of his injury.

4. Justice Stevens, dissenting: a rigid rule is unnecessary—all we need is a looser standard that can be applied on a case-by-case basis.

5. Why does the statute of limitations exist?[3]

    (a) Protect against the "cloud of litigation."

    (b) Protect against "stale claims."

    (c) Keep the plaintiff from sitting on his rights.

3.2 Due Process Requirements

1. Fifth Amendment: "No person shall be . . . deprived of life, liberty, or property, without due process of law."

2. Fourteenth Amendment: "No **State** shall . . . deprive any person of life, liberty, or property, without due process of law."

3.3 Remedies

1. **Plenary**: Usually awarded at the end of a lawsuit. Usual types: compensatory and punitive damages, injunctions, and declaratory judgments.

2. **Provisional**: Can be awarded at any time while a lawsuit is pending. Usual types: attachment (seizure of property), temporary restraining orders, preliminary injunctions. They are "designed to stabilize the situation pending the final disposition of the case or to provide security to the plaintiff so that if she succeeds in obtaining judgment she will be able to enforce it effectively."[4]

---

[3] Casebook pp. 54–55
[4] Casebook p. 46.

3.4 Notice and Opportunity to be Heard: *Fuentes v. Shevin*

Ex parte prejudgment and seizure requires notice and opportunity to be heard.

1. Do statutes that allow writs of replevin only upon ex parte application and posting of bond violate the Fourteenth Amendment?

2. In multiple consolidated cases, a creditor was granted an ex parte writ of replevin for the property of Fuentes, debtor in default (which statutes in Florida and Pennsylvania statutes allowed).

3. Justice Stewart: these statutes allowing ex parte attachment violate the Due Process Clause (Fourteenth Amendment). Absent extraordinary circumstances, due process requires **notice** and **opportunity to be heard** before deprivation.

4. Justice White, dissenting: "If there is a default, it would seem not only 'fair,' but essential, that the creditor be allowed to repossess; and I cannot say that the likelihood of a mistaken claim of default is sufficiently real or recurring to justify a broad constitutional requirement that a creditor do more than the typical state law requires him to do."[5]

5. Key due process protections: **notice** and **opportunity to be heard** (in a meaningful way).

6. *Mitchell v. W.T. Grant*: A similar statute in Louisiana was upheld on the grounds that (1) the applicant for the writ must declare the facts in a certified petition or affidavit, and (2) the showing must be made to a judge, not merely a court official.

7. *North Georgia Finishing, Inc. v. Di-Chem, Inc.*: A similar Georgia statute was struck down because (1) the affidavit can be filed by the petitioner's attorney, who need not have any direct knowledge of the facts of the dispute, and (2) the writ is issuable by a court clerk, not a judge.

8. The minimum constitutional requirements for valid ex parte prejudgment and seizure appear to be:

    (a) An application grounded in facts.

    (b) Issued by a judge, not a court official.

    (c) A speedy hearing.

    (d) Only applicable to a limited range of transactions.[6]

---

[5] Casebook p. 74.
[6] See California's version of these statues, casebook p. 82 top.

3.5 Deprivation and Due Process: *Connecticut v. Doehr*

Prejudgment attachment of real estate violates due process if it is without prior notice or hearing, without extraordinary circumstances, and without a bond.

1. Under a Connecticut statute, DiGiovanni won a $75,000 prejudgment attachment on Doehr's home in conjunction with a civil action for assault and battery.

2. Justice White: the Connecticut statute would allow deprivation for cases where the defendant's property claim would fail to convince a jury. Without exigent circumstances, a preattachment hearing is required.

3. Justices Marshall, Stevens, O'Connor, and White, concurring: bonds are also necessary in all cases.

4. Justice Rehnquist, concurring: liens can serve a useful purpose (e.g., for laborers to enforce their interests over delinquent landowners). Also, the terms "bond" and "exigent circumstances" are overly vague.

5. The *Matthews* test determines whether deprivation meets due process requirements:[7]

    (a) What are the private interests that deprivation will affect?

    (b) What is the risk of erroneous deprivation, and what safeguards are in place?

    (c) What is the interest of the party seeking the judgment remedy (in *Mathews* originally, this was the government; here it's the private plaintiff)?

---

[7] Casebook p. 85.

§ 4 Jurisdiction

1. **Territorial jurisdiction**: jurisdiction over cases arising in or involving people residing within a defined territory.

2. **Personal jurisdiction**: a court's power to bring a person into its adjudicative process.

3. **Subject matter jurisdiction**: the court's power to decide a particular type of case.

4. The Due Process Clause (Fourteenth Amendment) governs jurisdictional questions.

5. **Venue**: is this the right court within a proper jurisdiction in which to sue?

6. *Forum non conveniens*: is there a jurisdiction that is dramatically more appropriate?

7. Parties must raise objections to jurisdiction at the beginning of a suit.

8. A judgment **void when rendered is void forever** and is therefore vulnerable to **collateral attack**. *Pennoyer*.

4.1 Personal Jurisdiction

1. **Territorial power framework**: a court cannot establish personal jurisdicion over someone outside of its physical territory. *Pennoyer*.

2. States can require implied consent to jurisdiction from out-of-state drivers. *Hess*.

3. In personam jurisdiction is established if the defendant has **minimum contacts** with the forum state. *International Shoe*.

4. General vs. specific jurisdiction:

    (a) **General jurisdiction**: The defendant has substantial enough contacts with a state that any dispute can be litigated in that state, regardless of whether the dispute arises from those contacts.

    (b) **Specific jurisdiction**: Jurisdiction is based on contacts related to the specific dispute.[8]

    (c) A **stream of commerce** connection is insufficient to establish general jurisdiction. *Goodyear*.

---
[8]Casebook p. 186.

5. **Purposeful availment** means benefiting from the protection of the forum state's laws. See *World-Wide Volkswagen* below. Selling products that end up in the forum state is insufficient (*World-Wide Volkswagen*), but establishing a franchise relationship is enough (*Burger King*).

6. **Purposeful direction** establishes general jurisdiction, but it does not exist if the seller did not explicitly intend to sell products to the specific forum state. *J. McIntyre*.

7. **Long-arm statutes** authorize courts to exercise jurisdiction over people beyond their borders. See more below and *Bensusan*.

8. **Rule 4(k)**—federal personal jurisdiction analysis:

    (a) If the claim arises under *state* law, apply the state long-arm statute.

    (b) Is there a federal long-arm statute? If so, apply it and check whether the defendant has minimum contacts with the US. (If there is no personal jurisdiction in any state, you can sue in any district court.) If not, apply the state long-arm statute.

9. Quasi in rem jurisdiction is also based on the minimum contacts test, not the territorial power framework. *Shaffer*.

10. **Physical presence** establishes personal jurisdiction. *Burnham*. Property does not. *Shaffer*.

11. Due process requires **notice and opportunity to be heard**. *Mullane*. The government must take affirmative steps to ensure adequate notice (*Flowers*).

12. **Forum selection clauses** in contracts of adhesion are enforceable means of establishing personal jurisdiction. *Carnival Cruise Lines*.

4.1.1 Territorial Power: *Pennoyer v. Neff*

Under the territorial power framework of personal jurisdiction, a court cannot establish jurisdiction over someone beyond its physical borders.

1. Mitchell sued Neff in Oregon state court for nonpayment of legal fees rendered in 1862–1863. Neff was nowhere to be found, so Mitchell published notice of the suit in the *Pacific Christian Advocate*.

2. Neff did not appear, so the court granted a default judgment for Mitchell.

3. Neff's property in Oregon was attached and then sold at auction to Mitchell, who then sold it to Pennoyer.

4. Eight years later, Neff turned up and sued Pennoyer to recover the property.

5. Justice Field:

    (a) The basis for personal jurisdiction is a state's territorial power. States are all-powerful within their borders and powerless beyond.

    (b) Service by publication was insufficient to establish personal jurisdiction over a non-resident in an in personam suit (thought it would suffice for in personam suits). Thus, the original judgment against Neff was void.

    (c) Doctrine of **collateral attack**: a judgment void when rendered is void forever.

6. *Milliken v. Meyer*: domicile within a state is sufficient to establish jurisdiction.

4.1.2 Jurisdiction Over Out-of-State Drivers: *Hess v. Pawloski*

States can implement statutes requiring out-of-state drivers to give implied consent to personal jurisdiction within that state.

1. Hess, a Pennsylvania resident, "negligently and wantonly drove a motor vehicle on a public highway in Massachusetts," causing injury to Pawloski.[9]

2. Pawloski brought a negligence suit in Massachusetts state court. Hess contested personal jurisdiction. Denied. Hess appealed on Fourteenth Amendment grounds.

3. Justice Butler:

    (a) In earlier cases (e.g., *Kane v. New Jersey*), the Court upheld the constitutionality of statutes requiring out-of-state drivers to appoint an agent to receive service of process.

    (b) States can legitimately require drivers to appoint similar agent implicitly, and these kinds of statutes do not not constitute discrimination against non-residents.

    (c) Therefore, it is consistent with due process for states to require out-of-state drivers to implicitly appoint an agent to receive process, thereby establishing jurisdiction over those drivers if civil actions arise.

    (d) Affirmed.

---

[9] 274 U.S. 352, 353 (1927).

4.1.3 Minimum Contacts: *International Shoe Co. v. Washington*

"But now that the capias ad respondendum has given way to personal service of summons or other form of notice, due process requires only that in order to subject a defendant to a judgment in personam, if he be not present within the territory of the forum, he have certain '**minimum contacts with it such that the maintenance of the suit does not offend 'traditional notions of fair play and substantial justice.'**"[10]

1. The State of Washington sued International Shoe to recover unpaid contributions to the state unemployment compensation fund.

2. Justice Stone:

    (a) International Shoe argued first that the Washington statute imposed an unconstitutional burden on interstate commerce. The court rejected International Shoe's argument on the basis that "it is no longer debatable" that the commerce clause gives Congress broad power to regulate interstate commerce.

    (b) Second, International Shoe argued that merely soliciting orders within a state "does not render the seller amenable to suit within the state." Historically, physical presence within a state was a prerequisite for jurisdiction in in personam cases (*Pennoyer*). But now, **minimum contacts** are sufficient.

    (c) "Presence" is a symbolic term that can refer to business activities within a territory. It can refer to activities that give rise to the liabilities at issue in the suit. Moreover, since an entity enjoys certain benefits and protections from a state's laws, it also has an obligation to that state.

    (d) Washington was entitled to recover the unpaid contributions.

3. Justice Black, concurring: states have a constitutional power to tax and sue corporations that do business in the state's territory. The test of "fair play and substantial justice," however, is "confusing" and gives the court the unwarranted power to strike down any legislation it might see as violating "natural justice."

4.1.4 Purposeful Availment: *World-Wide Volkswagen Corp. v. Woodson*

Selling a product that ends up in another state is insufficient to establish personal jurisdiction over the seller, because the seller has not purposefully availed itself of the benefits of doing business in the forum state.

1. The Robinsons bought an Audi in New York. It caught fire in an accident in Oklahoma. They brought a products liability action in Oklahoma state

---

[10] Casebook p. 179.

court against every link in the distribution chain. The regional distributor (World-Wide Volkswagen) and retailer (Seaway) contested Oklahoma's jurisdiction.

2. Justice White:

   (a) To establish jurisdiction, defendants must have minimum contacts with the forum state and jurisdiction must not violate "traditional notions of fair play and substantial justice" (*International Shoe*).

   (b) Elements of "fair play and substantial justice" include:[11]

       i. The forum State's interest in adjudicating the dispute.
       ii. The convenience of the venue for the plaintiff.
       iii. The interstate judicial system's interest in efficient resolution.
       iv. States' shared interest in fundamental policy goals.

   (c) Jurisdictional rules have been relaxed since *Pennoyer*, but the Constitution nonetheless privileges state sovereignty.

   (d) "Petitioners [World-Wide and Seaway] carry on no activity whatsoever in Oklahoma."[12]

   (e) Petitioners could not reasonably predict being haled into court in Oklahoma. Corporations can "purposely avail" themselves of the benefits of conducting activity in the forum state—but there is no such availment here.[13] Were it otherwise, "[e]very seller of chattels would in effect appoint the chattel his agent for service of process."[14]

   (f) No contacts, so no jurisdiction.

3. Justice Brennan, dissenting: The Court reads *International Shoe* too narrowly. The seller and dealer purposefully injected their product "into the stream of interstate commerce," thus establishing minimum contacts.[15]

4. Justices Marshall, dissenting: The dealer and seller chose to become part of a global marketing and servicing network. Cars derive their value from being mobile. The dealer and seller received economic advantage from the ability to draw revenue from Oklahoma.

5. Justice Blackmun, dissenting: It is confusing why the distributor and seller are getting sued here. Also, cars are mobile by nature.

---

[11] Casebook p. 190.
[12] Casebook p. 192.
[13] Casebook p. 194.
[14] Casebook p. 193.
[15] Casebook p. 196.

4.1.5 Purposeful Availment II: *Burger King Corp. v. Rudzewicz*

Establishing a franchise relationship with an out-of-state corporation is sufficient to constitute purposeful availment.

1. Rudcewicz and MacShara operated a Burger King franchise in Michigan. They fell behind on their payments. Burger King, based in Florida, sued them in Florida district court for breaching their franchise obligations and for trademark infringement.

2. The defendants moved to dismiss for lack of personal jurisdiction. The district court denied the motion, holding that the Florida long-arm statute established jurisdiction over disputes arising from the franchise agreement. The district court then found for Burger King.

3. The Eleventh Circuit reversed, holding that the defendants did not have reasonable notice and were "financially unprepared" for litigation in a Florida forum.[16]

4. Justice Brennan:

    (a) The "fair warning" requirement is satisfied if the defendant "**purposefully avails** itself of the privilege of conducting activities in the forum state, thus invoking the benefit of the protection of its laws."[17]

    (b) Once minimum contacts are established, the court may consider other factors:[18]

    　i. "the burden on the defendant"

    　ii. "the forum state's interest in adjudicating the dispute"

    　iii. "the plaintiff's interest in obtaining the most efficient resolution of controversies"

    　iv. the "shared interest of the several States in furthering fundamental substantive social policies"

    (c) Rudcewicz established a substantial relationship with the Florida headquarters and did not show how jurisdiction would be fundamentally unfair. Reversed.

5. Justice Stevens, dissenting: it is fundamentally unfair to require a franchisee to submit to jurisdiction in the district of the franchisor. There is a huge disparity in bargaining power, and franchises almost always limit their activities to local markets.

6. In *Calder* (the *National Enquirer* libel case), the Court developed the "effects test," under which activities "purposefully directed" at a state can establish jurisdiction.

---

[16] Casebook p. 213.
[17] Casebook p. 215.
[18] Casebook p. 217; cf. *World-Wide Volkswagen*.

(a) Bradt on *Calder*: California actress Shirley Jones (of "Partridge Family" fame) sued the National Enquirer for libel based on a story it published essentially calling her a drunk. Jones sued in California state court. The Enquirer, which is based in Florida, contested jurisdiction on the ground that it did not have minimum contacts with California. The reporter had only gone to CA once, and everything else was essentially done in Florida. The Supreme Court held that there *was* personal jurisdiction over the Enquirer in California on the ground that it "expressly aimed" its conduct toward California. This is an interesting spin on purposeful availment commonly referred to as the "effects test"—if a defendant commits an intentional tort aimed at the forum state and causes harm in the forum state, there is specific jurisdiction over the defendant in cases arising out of that harm in the forum state. In *Calder*, the Court found that the Enquirer had aimed its conduct at California because (a) it knew that's where Jones lived and worked and would therefore suffer the brunt of the injury, and (b) because California was the largest state for circulation of the Enquirer, so it knew the harm in that state would be significant.

7. Purposeful direction is distinct from purposeful availment, which is the quid pro quo the Court recognized in *International Shoe*: the privilege of enjoying "the benefits and protections of the laws" of a state gives rise to obligations, including to the procedure of responding to a suit in that state.[19]

4.1.6 Defenses to Personal Jurisdiction

1. Default and collaterally attack (*Pennoyer*).

2. Appear in court, move to dismiss, and appeal if you lose (*International Shoe*).

4.1.7 General and Specific Jurisdiction: *Goodyear Dunlop Tires Operations, S.A. v. Brown*

A "stream of commerce" connection to the forum state is insufficient to establish personal jurisdiction.

1. A bus accident outside Paris killed two 13-year-old boys from North Carolina. The parents sued Goodyear USA and three of its foreign subsidiaries in North Carolina state court.

2. The subsidiaries moved to dismiss for lack of personal jurisdiction. The North Carolina trial court denied the motion, the appellate court affirmed, and the state Supreme Court denied review.

---

[19]Casebook p. 238.

4　JURISDICTION

3. Justice Ginsburg:

    (a) **General jurisdiction** exists when an actor has "continuous and systematic" affiliations with the forum state.[20]

    (b) **Specific jurisdiction** exists when the specific cause of action is connected to the forum state.

    (c) A limited "stream of commerce" connection to the forum state is insufficient to establish personal jurisdiction.

    (d) Reversed.

4.1.8　Product Distribution and Purposeful Direction: *J. McIntyre Machinery, Ltd. v. Nicastro*

Distributing products indirectly to the forum state is insufficient to establish personal jurisdiction without purposeful direction or purposeful availment.

1. Nicastro injured his hand while using a machine that J. McIntyre, an English corporation, manufactured. Nicastro sued J. McIntyre in New Jersey state court.

2. The New Jersey Supreme Court held that "New Jersey's courts can exercise jurisdiction over a foreign manufacturer of a product so long as the manufacturer 'knows or reasonable should know that its products are distributed through a nationwide distribution system.'"[21]

3. Justice Kennedy: J. McIntyre did not purposefully direct its activities at New Jersey, nor did it purposefully avail itself of the privilege of the benefits and protections of New Jersey's laws. Reversed.

4. Justice Breyer, concurring: this case can be decided on precedent alone. There is no need to update jurisdictional rules to account for developments in modern commerce.

5. Justice Ginsburg, dissenting: J. McIntyre used a distributor to shield itself from liability, but it clearly intended to market its products to the United States as a whole.

4.1.9　Long-Arm Statutes

1. "A court will not find in personam jurisdiction unless there is statutory authorization for the exercise of that jurisdiction."[22]

2. Long-arm statutes enable states to assert jurisdiction beyond their borders.

---

[20]Supplement p. 4.
[21]Supplement p. 15.
[22]Casebook p. 241.

3. Some extend jurisdiction to the full extent that the Constitution allows. Others specify the circumstances in which states can extend jurisdiction.

4. Detailed long-arm statutes can make the law more predictable.

5. Federal courts usually follow the long-arm statutes of the states in which they sit.

6. If the state long-arm statute does not extend to the full constitutional limits of in personam jurisdiction, the only question before the court is statutory (e.g., in *Bensusan*, below).

4.1.10 Online Activity and Long-Arm Statutes: *Bensusan Rest. Corp v. King*

Digital activity complicates jurisdictional questions, but long-arm statutes still place enforceable limits on personal jurisdiction.

1. Bensusan and King both owned cabarets named "Blue Note" in New York City and Columbia, MO, respectively. King built a website using the name. Bensusan sued in the Southern District of New York for compensatory damages, punitive damages, costs, attorney's fees, and to enjoin King from using the name.

2. The New York long-arm statute[23] required that the defendant must have been physically present in the state when he committed the act in question.

3. The district court rejected Bensusan's complaint under FRCP 12(b)(2) for lack of personal jurisdiction. The Second Circuit affirmed, holding that King was not physically present and did not meet any of the other statutory requirements for establishing jurisdiction.

4. Federal court cannot be an authoritative source of state law—it can only infer what New York courts would do in a comparable case.

5. In *Inset Systems, Inc. v. Instruction Set, Inc.*, a Connecticut district court held that advertising online could potentially reach "as many as 10,000 Internet users within Connecticut" and was "continuously available." Therefore, the advertiser had "purposefully availed itself of the privileges of doing business in Connecticut."[24]

6. The **Zippo test**: in *Zippo Manufacturing Co. v. Zippo Dot Com, Inc.*, Zippo (the lighter company) sued Zippo (the publishing company) in Pennsylvania district court for state and federal trademark claims. The court established the Zippo test for determining jurisdiction in Internet cases. The test relies on a scale of commercial activity. On one side of the scale are sites that exist exclusively to do business online. If a defendant

---

[23] N.Y.C.P.L.R. § 320(a).
[24] Casebook p. 250.

knowingly enters into a contract with residents of a foreign jurisdiction, then personal jurisdiction is proper. On the other side of the scale are sites that passively post information. Personal jurisdiction cannot be asserted for those sites. In the middle are sites in which the user can exchange information with a host computer. In those cases, the "level of interaction" and the "commercial nature of the exchange" are the grounds for determining the exercise of jurisdiction.

4.1.11 FRCP 4(k): Territorial Limits of Effective Service

- (1) Framework for exercising jurisdiction over defendants in general.
    - (A) The state's long-arm statute governs absent a contrary federal rule or statute.
    - (B) "Bulge" jurisdiction: third-party defendants are subject to in personam jurisdiction if they can be served within 100 miles of where the summons was issued.
    - (C) Courts can exercise any in personam jurisdiction that a federal statute authorizes.
- (2) Framework for exercising jurisdiction in federal courts.

4.1.12 Challenging the *Pennoyer* Framework for Quasi In Rem Actions: *Shaffer v. Heitner*

Jurisdiction in quasi in rem actions must be based on the minimum contacts test (*International Shoe*), not the territorial power framework (*Pennoyer*). Owning stock in a corporation incorporated in the forum state does not meet the minimum contacts requirement.

1. Heitner owned one share of stock in Greyhound Corp., a Delaware corporation with its primary place of business in Phoenix. Heitner sued 28 of Greyhound's officers and directors in Delaware state court for damages in a case involving antitrust and criminal contempt violations in Oregon. Under a Delaware statute, he filed for an order of sequestration against the property of the officers. The property consisted of Greyhound options and 82,000 shares of common stock.

2. The defendants argued that the sequestration statute did not satisfy due process and that the property seized could not be attached in Delaware. Denied.

3. Justice Marshall:
    (a) *Quasi in rem* jurisdiction has traditionally been based on physical presence (*Pennoyer*), not minimum contacts.
    (b) The *Pennoyer* framework included a few exceptions (marriage, foreign corporations doing business in a state, etc.).

(c) Modern realities expanded the *Pennoyer* framework (e.g., *Hess*) without fundamentally changing it.

(d) The *International Shoe* framework supplanted *Pennoyer* for *in personam* cases. No similar conceptual revision has occurred for *in rem* cases, though lower courts have moved strongly in that direction.

(e) Key break from *Pennoyer*: asserting jurisdiction over a thing is a "customarily elliptical way" of asserting jurisdiction over the interests of a person in a thing.

(f) *Pennoyer* led to odd situations where property served as the basis for jurisdiction in causes of action completely unrelated to the property (like the present case). It was illogical, though *Pennoyer* permitted it, to assert jurisdiction indirectly, via property, if direct assertion of personal jurisdiction would not be allowed.

(g) There are no good historical reasons to cling to *Pennoyer*.

(h) We should therefore use the *International Shoe* test for all assertions of state court jurisdiction.

(i) Appellants' holdings did not constitute minimum contacts with Delaware—thus, Delaware did not have jurisdiction.

(j) Reversed.

4. Justice Powell, concurring:

(a) Property that is "indisputably and permanently" within a state (e.g., real estate) might pass the *International Shoe* test. The court should reserve judgment on that issue.

5. Justice Stevens, concurring:

(a) Fair notice requires warning that a particular activity will open the actor to the jurisdiction of a foreign sovereign. Buying stock includes no such warning.

(b) Agree with Powell.

(c) There are other longstanding methods of asserting jurisdiction based on territory that should not be discounted.

6. Justice Brennan, concurring in part and dissenting in part:

(a) Delaware explicitly did not enact a law basing *quasi in rem* jurisdiction over shareholders on a minimum contacts test. For the court to invalidate this imaginary statute is a pure "advisory opinion."

4.1.13 Physical Presence and Personal Jurisdiction: *Burnham v. Superior Court of Cal.*

Presence within a state is sufficient to establish personal jurisdiction.

4 JURISDICTION

1. Burnham and his wife decided to separate. Before his wife moved to California, the couple agreed to divorce on grounds of "irreconcilable differences." After she left, however, Burnham filed for divorce on grounds of "desertion."

2. His wife brought suit in California. Some months later, Burnham was on a business trip in California, where he was served with court summons and a divorce petition.

3. Burnham filed a motion to quash on the argument that his brief contacts with California did not meet the requirements to establish jurisdiction. The Superior Court denied the motion and the Court of Appeal denied mandamus relief.

4. Justice Scalia:

    (a) The question is whether physical presence is enough to establish jurisdiction or whether the person must also have minimum contacts.

    (b) There has never been a case that suggests in-state service is insufficient to establish personal jurisdiction.

    (c) The *Pennoyer* territorial power framework had been broadened over the 20th century. *International Shoe* established a different standard.

    (d) Burnham sought to establish that presence in the forum state is no longer sufficient to establish jurisdiction. This was entirely wrong. The *International Shoe* test was developed by analogy to the "physical presence" test, and it would be "perverse" to use the *Shoe* test to undermine it.

    (e) *Shaffer* involved an absent defendant, and it held that the defendant's contacts must include property related to the litigation to establish jurisdiction (or, in a different light, that quasi in rem and in personam are really one and the same). There was no absent defendant in the present case.

    (f) In response to Brennan's concurrence: (1) Brennan proposes a standard based on "contemporary notions of due process"—but this is hopelessly subjective. (2) Brennan argues that the concept of transient jurisdiction—of presence within a state creating a "reasonable expectation" of being subject to suit—is based on fairness. Really, though, it's based on the same traditions that Brennan tries to dismiss. "Justice Brennan's long journey is a circular one."

    (g) Affirmed.

5. Justice White, concurring: it would be unworkable to decide in each case whether service was delivered fairly. The rule should stand as-is.

6. Justice Brennan, concurring:

- (a) A rule does not comport with due process simply because of its pedigree.
- (b) *Shaffer* established that all rules, regardless of pedigree, must comport with modern understandings of due process.
- (c) More than a century of the rule's existence gives defendants ample notice that their presence within a state can subject them to that state's jurisdiction.
- (d) By visiting a state, a defendant avails himself of that state's benefits. Without the transient jurisdiction rule, the actor would have the full benefit of access to the state's courts as a plaintiff while remaining immune from the same courts' jurisdiction. This asymmetry would be unfair.

7. Justice Stevens, concurring: the other justices' opinions are overly broad.

4.1.14 "Notice Reasonably Calculated" *Mullane v. Central Hanover Bank & Trust*

If it's easy to serve notice by mail or in person, notice by publication does not satisfy due process requirements. "An elementary and fundamental requirement of due process in any proceeding which is to be accorded finality is **notice reasonably calculated**, under all the circumstances, to apprise interested parties of the pendency of the action and afford them an **opportunity to present their objections**."

1. A New York law required a judicial settlement of a common trust fund. In strict compliance with the statute, the Central Hanover Bank and Trust gave notice to beneficiaries by publication in a local newspaper.

2. Mullane was appointed special guardian for parties with an interest in the fund. He argued that notice by publication violated the Fourteenth Amendment's requirement for notice of judicial proceedings.

3. The NY Court of Appeals rejected Mullane's argument.

4. Justice Jackson:
   - (a) The only notice to beneficiaries appeared in a local newspaper, in strict compliance with the NY statute.
   - (b) At the time of the first investment, the trust had contacted each person by mail.
   - (c) It doesn't matter whether this proceeding was in rem, quasi in rem, or in personam. In all cases, courts have the right to protect claimants' rights to notice and hearing and determine claimants' interests.
   - (d) Notice by publication is chancy at best compared to notice in person—"we are unable to regard this as more than a feint."

4 JURISDICTION

(e) It's not necessary to put huge effort into finding unknown claimants. Notice by publication is fine if it's not reasonably easy to make contact.

(f) For parties with known contact information, notice by mail is the minimum requirement. The NY statute requiring a minimum of notice by publication in all cases is unconstitutional.

4.1.15 Service by Mail: *Jones v. Flowers*

When notice served by certified mail is returned undelivered, the government must take additional reasonable steps (e.g., service by regular mail or posting at the physical address) to satisfy due process.

1. The plaintiff, Jones, was delinquent on his property taxes. The state sent two certified letters to his address over the course of two years, both of which were returned as "unclaimed." Just before the property was to be auctioned, the state also published a notice of public sale in a newspaper. The house was sold to Flowers.

2. Jones sued Flowers and the Commissioner, arguing that failure to provide notice of the tax sale violated due process. The trial court granted summary judgment in favor of the defendants. The Arkansas Supreme Court affirmed.

3. Justice Roberts:

    (a) Due process does not require that the property owner receive actual notice, but it does require a reasonable attempt (*Mullane*).

    (b) A person who actually wanted to inform someone about an impending tax sale would surely take extra steps if a certified letter of notice was returned unclaimed.

    (c) The state could have resent the letter by regular mail or posted it physically at the address. (It should not be required, though, to hunt for Jones's contact information.)

    (d) Reversed.

4. Justice Thomas, dissenting: process requirements must be determined ex ante. They should not be dependent on the outcome of the first attempt.

4.1.16 Contractual Consent to Jurisdiction: *Carnival Cruise Lines, Inc. v. Shrute*

Forum selection clauses in contracts of adhesion are enforceable. Plaintiffs have a high burden of proof to show that a forum is so inconvenient that it violates due process.

1. The plaintiffs, the Shutes, purchased tickets through a travel agent for a seven-day cruise. The cruise line, Carnival, sent the defendants the tickets by mail. The tickets included a contract that named Florida as the forum state for any litigation regarding the contract. By purchasing the tickets, the Shutes agreed to the terms of the contract.

2. During the cruise, Mrs. Shute slipped on a mat and injured herself. The Shutes sued for negligence in the Western District of Washington. Carnival argued that (1) the forum selection clause in the contract required the Shutes to bring suit in Florida, and (2) Carnival did not have sufficient contacts with Washington to allow its courts to exercise personal jurisdiction.

3. The district court granted Carnival's motion to dismiss on the grounds that Carnival had insufficient contacts with Washington to exercise personal jurisdiction.

4. The Ninth Circuit reversed on the grounds that Mrs. Shute would not have been injured but for Carnival's solicitation of business in Washington. It further held that the forum selection clause could not be enforced because (1) it was not freely bargained for, (2) the Shutes were physically and financially incapable of pursuing litigation in Florida, and (3) the clause violated the Limitation of Vessel Owner's Liability Act.

5. Issues before the Supreme Court:

    (a) Was the forum selection clause enforceable?

    (b) Was it too inconvenient for the Shutes to pursue litigation in Florida?

    (c) Did the forum selection clause violate the Limitation of Vessel Owner's Liability Act?

6. Justice Blackmun:

    (a) In their briefs, the Shutes conceded that they received adequate notice of the forum selection clause.

    (b) Some forum selection clauses might not be enforceable, e.g., if they were established through "fraud or overreaching."

    (c) In *The Bremen*, the court upheld the validity of a forum selection clause in international admiralty between two commercial actors. The Ninth Circuit applied *The Bremen* in this case to hold that the forum selection clause was unenforceable because the parties had not negotiated it. The Supreme Court (Blackmun here) reasoned that the Shutes (individuals) did not negotiate with Carnival (a large corporation).

    (d) However, the lack of bargaining does not automatically invalidate the contract. There are plenty of reasons why a non-negotiated forum selection clause would be reasonable: (1) to avoid litigation in every single passenger's different forum, (2) to dispel confusion about the proper forum, and (3) to reduce fares resulting from the limited fora. Thus, the clause is enforceable.

   (e) Re Florida as an inconvenient forum: Shutes have not satisfied the burden of proof to show heavy inconvenience.

   (f) Re violation of the Limitation of Vessel Owner's Liability Act: there is no evidence that Congress intended to avoid having a plaintiff travel to a distant forum in order to litigate.

   (g) The forum selection clause was enforceable. Reversed.

7. Justice Stevens, dissenting:

   (a) Only the most meticulous passenger will be aware of the forum selection clause.

   (b) Passengers will not be able to evaluate the contract until they agree to it by purchasing a non-refundable ticket. Negotiation is logically impossible.

   (c) The forum selection clause *is* null and void under the Limitation of Vessel Owner's Liability Act.

   (d) This is a contract of adhesion. The Shutes did not know or consent to all of its terms.

   (e) Forum selection clauses are not enforceable if they were not freely bargained for.

   (f) The forum selection clause makes it more difficult for the Shutes to recover damages for the slip-and-fall, which is contrary to public policy.

8. Before *Carnival*, forum selection clauses in form contracts were disfavored. Now they're found in virtually every consumer contract.

4.2 Subject Matter Jurisdiction and Venue

1. Federal courts have **limited jurisdiction**. Cases must be within their limited subject matter jurisdiction. State courts have **general jurisdiction**.

2. The two types of subject matter jurisdiction we deal with are **federal question** and **diversity** (see each section below).

3. The primary sources of limits on subject matter jurisdiction are Article III of the Constitution, federal jurisdictional statutes, and state long-arm statutes.

4. Unlike personal jurisdiction, **subject matter jurisdiction cannot be waived**, because waiver would upset the structural balance between state

and federal courts. Parties can raise subject matter jurisdiction issues at any point, and courts can raise it *sua sponte* (as the Supreme Court did in *Mottley*).

5. Federal courts must find that they have subject matter jurisdiction before they can decide any question on the merits.[25]

4.2.1 Federal Question Jurisdiction

1. Article III authorizes the federal judiciary: " . . . The judicial power shall extend to all cases, in law and equity, **arising under this Constitution, the laws of the United States**, and treaties made, or which shall be made, under their authority;—to all cases affecting ambassadors, other public ministers and consuls;—to all cases of admiralty and maritime jurisdiction;—to controversies to which the United States shall be a party;—to controversies between two or more states;—between a state and citizens of another state;—**between citizens of different states**;—between citizens of the same state claiming lands under grants of different states, and between a state, or the citizens thereof, and foreign states, citizens or subjects . . . ."

2. Federal judicial powers are **enumerated**, just like federal legislative powers. But unlike congressional power, the scope of the judiciary is narrowly construed.[26]

3. **28 U.S.C § 1331 establishes federal question jurisdiction**: "The district courts shall have original jurisdiction of all civil actions arising under the Constitution, laws, or treaties of the United States."

4. **States have concurrent jurisdiction over cases based on federal law** unless Congress has provided for exclusive jurisdiction.[27]

5. **Federal courts have concurrent jurisdiction over state law cases** as long as there is subject matter jurisdiction. Diversity is typically the basis for federal subject matter jurisdiction, though federal questions are also often involved.[28]

6. Article III is broad—federal courts can hear a case as long as there is a federal "ingredient" involved.[29]

---

[25] Casebook p. 448.
[26] Casebook p. 372 n. 2.
[27] Casebook p. 373.
[28] Casebook p. 373–374.
[29] "We think, then, that when a question to which the judicial power of the Union is extended by the constitution, forms an ingredient of the original cause, it is in the power of Congress to give the Circuit Courts jurisdiction of that cause, although other questions of fact or of law may be involved in it." *Osborn v. Bank of U.S.*, 22 U.S. 738, 823 (1824).

4 JURISDICTION

7. Federal cases must be based on **well pleaded complaints**, i.e., an anticipated federal defense is not sufficient to establish federal question jurisdiction. *Mottley*.

8. Even if there is no federal cause of action, federal courts can choose to hear state law causes if they **implicate significant federal issues**. *Grable*.

9. Complaints must satisfy the **well-pleaded complaint rule**. *Mottley*.

10. Courts can hear state law issues if they **implicate significant federal issues**. *Grable*.

4.2.1.1 Well Pleaded Complaint: *Louisville & Nashville R.R. Co. v. Mottley*

Well pleaded complaint rule: "Plaintiff may not anticipate a federal defense by the defendant in her complaint and use that defense as a basis for federal jurisdiction."[30]

1. Facts:
   (a) September 1871: plaintiffs won a judgment against the railroad company that awarded them free rail passes for life.
   (b) June 29, 1906: Congress passed a statute forbidding free passes or free transportation.
   (c) January 1, 1907: the railroad company stopped honoring the plaintiffs' free passes.

2. The Mottleys brought a contract action against the railroad in federal court, alleging that (1) the congressional statute does not cover their kind of pass and (2) if the statute did cover their kind of pass, it would violate the Fifth Amendment.

3. The Supreme Court held that there was no subject matter question in this case. Both parties were citizens of Kentucky, so there was no diversity jurisdiction. The plaintiff's claim was based solely on a private contract, and although the plaintiffs anticipated a federal defense from the defendants, the court held that **an anticipated federal defense is not sufficient to establish federal question jurisdiction**.

4.2.1.2 The Kaleidoscope and the Welcome Mat: *Grable & Sons Metal Prods. v. Darue Eng. & Manuf.*

A federal cause of action is not always required to establish federal question jurisdiction. Courts can choose to hear state law cases if they "implicate significant federal issues."

---
[30] Casebook p. 378.

4 JURISDICTION

1. 1994: The IRS seized Grable's land in Michigan to satisfy its tax delinquency. It notified Grable by mail and sold the property to Darue under a quitclaim deed.

2. 1999: Grable brought a quiet title action against Darue in state court, claiming that Darue's title was invalid because the IRS failed to notify Grable with personal service as required by statute.

3. Darue removed to federal court on the basis that Grable's claim depended on an interpretation of federal tax law. The district court declined to remand to state court. It granted summary judgment in favor of Darue, holding that the IRS had substantially (if not literally) complied with the statute.

4. The Sixth Circuit affirmed the summary judgment. It held that jurisdiction existed because (1) the title claim raised an issue of federal law and (2) the claim implicated a substantial federal interest in construing federal tax law.

5. The question before the Supreme Court was whether a federal cause of action is always required to establish federal question jurisdiction.

6. Justice Souter:

    - Federal jurisdiction exists for state law claims if they "implicate significant federal issues."[31]

    - District courts can refuse to exercise jurisdiction if the cause of action is not based on a federal question and there is no diversity of citizenship.

    - Justice Cardozo: "a request to exercise federal-question jurisdiction over a state action calls for a 'common-sense accommodation of judgment to [the] kaleidoscopic situations' that present a federal issue, in 'a selective process which picks the substantial causes out of the web and lays the other ones aside.'"[32]

    - "... the question is, does a state-law claim necessarily raise a stated federal issue, actually disputed and substantial, which a federal forum may entertain without disturbing any congressionally approved balance of federal and state judicial responsibilities."[33]

    - The Court saw the absence of a federal cause of action "not as a missing federal door key, always required, but as a missing welcome mat, required in the circumstances ..."[34]

    - Affirmed.

---

[31] Casebook p. 390.
[32] Casebook p. 391.
[33] Casebook p. 392.
[34] Casebook p. 394.

4 JURISDICTION

7. Justice Thomas, concurring:

   - Justice Holmes in *Merrill Dow* argued in his dissent that a federal cause of action should be necessary, not merely sufficient. Thomas argued that the current rule is unclear, and under the right circumstances he would be "willing to consider" adopting the clearer Holmes rule.[35]

4.2.2 Diversity Jurisdiction

1. Article III § 2 defines federal judicial jurisdiction to include "all Cases . . . between Citizens of different States . . . "

2. **28 U.S.C. § 1332 authorizes diversity jurisdiction**. Federal courts have original jurisdiction over all cases where the amount in controversy is greater than $75,000 and the parties meet the diversity requirements.

3. **Complete diversity** requires that none of the plaintiffs can be from the same state as any of the defendants. *Mas*.

4. One reason for establishing diversity jurisdiction was to protect out-of-state parties from prejudice in state courts.

5. Unlike subject matter jurisdiction, which did not receive permanent congressional authorization until 1875, Congress immediately granted diversity jurisdiction.

6. Plaintiffs' claims must meet the **amount in controversy** requirements (currently, $75,000). A plaintiff can aggregate multiple claims against a defendant to meet the amount in controversy requirement—however, a plaintiff cannot aggregate multiple claims against multiple defendants.

7. Corporations are citizens of their state of **incorporation** and the state where their **"nerve center"** is located. *Hertz*.

4.2.2.1 Complete Diversity: *Mas v. Perry*

Complete diversity requires that none of the plaintiffs can be from the same state as any of the defendants.

1. Mr. and Mrs. Mas were graduate assistants at Louisiana State University. They discovered that their landlord, Perry, had been spying on them through two-way mirrors for several months.

2. The plaintiffs sued Perry in district court in Louisiana. Perry moved to dismiss for lack of jurisdiction on the grounds that (1) the plaintiffs failed to prove diversity jurisdiction (because Mr. and Mrs. Mas lived in Louisiana) and (2) the jurisdictional amount of damages was lacking. The district court rejected the motion.

---
[35] Casebook p. 395–96.

4 JURISDICTION

3. The Fifth Circuit held:
   (a) Mr. Mas was a French resident, so there was diversity jurisdiction for his claim under 28 U.S.C. § 1332(a)(2) ("alienage jurisdiction").
   (b) Mrs. Mas was a domiciliary of Mississippi, so there was diversity jurisdiction for her claim under 28 U.S. § 1332(a)(1). (Domicile is distinct from residency. Although Mrs. Mas resided in Louisiana, she was a domiciliary of Mississippi, so diversity was preserved. Domicile is established when a person intends to remain in a state indefinitely.)
   (c) The amount in controversy well exceeded the threshold for federal jurisdiction (then $10,000). The **St. Paul Mercury** rule (or the "legal certainty" rule) requires defendants opposing jurisdiction to prove a "legal certainty" that the plaintiff could not recovery more than the statutory threshold (now $75,000, then $10,000).
   (d) Affirmed.

4.2.2.2 The Corporate Nerve Center: *Hertz Corp. v. Friend*

A corporation is a citizen where it is incorporated and where its "officers direct, control, and coordinate the corporation's activities."

1. The plaintiffs brought an class action claim against Hertz in California state court. Hertz requested removal to federal court. The plaintiffs argued that diversity jurisdiction was lacking because Hertz was a California citizen.

2. 28 U.S.C. § 1332(c)(1) provides that a corporation is a citizen of the state where it is incorporated *and* the state where it has its principle place of business.

3. Hertz argued that its principle place of business was New Jersey.[36] The district court disagreed, relying on a Ninth Circuit precedent that defines a corporation's principle place of business as the state where the amount of business it conducts is "significantly larger" than other states. It remanded to the state courts. The Ninth Circuit affirmed.

4. The Second Circuit rule was that a corporation's principle place of business is where its "nerve center" is located.[37]. Courts have interpreted the test with increasing complexity. The Supreme Court here sought to establish a simple rule. Expanding on the "nerve center" approach, it held that the principle place of business is "the place where a corporation's officers direct, control, and coordinate the corporation's activities."[38]

5. Under the Supreme Court's rule, Hertz's principle place of business was not California. Reversed.

---
[36] It is incorporated in Delaware.
[37] Supplement pp. 39–40.
[38] Supplement p. 41.

4.3 Supplemental Jurisdiction

1. Supplemental jurisdiction **allows a claim without jurisdiction to join a claim with valid jurisdiction**.

2. **28 U.S.C. § 1367**, passed in 1990, codified the federal common law rules of pendent and ancillary jurisdiction into the single concept of supplemental jurisdiction.

3. The court has **discretion not to exercise supplemental jurisdiction** under 28 U.S.C. § 1367(c).

4. Evaluating supplemental jurisdiction cases:

    (a) Is there a claim with valid original jurisdiction?

    (b) Do supplemental claims form part of the **same case or controversy?** 28 U.S.C. § 1367(a).

    (c) Are the supplemental claims **within the § 1367(b) rules?** A supplemental claim against a third-party defendant is not allowed if (1) the original basis for jurisdiction is diversity and (2) the supplemental claim would destroy diversity. § 1367(b) exists to prevent plaintiffs from bringing suit against diverse defendants and waiting for them to implead a non-diverse defendant who is the real target of the action. See *Owen*.

5. *Gibbs*'s "common nucleus of operative fact" requirement is preserved in § 1367(a) as the "same case or controversy."

6. *Kroger* is preserved in § 1367(b) as the limitation on supplemental jurisdiction for claims against third-party defendants where the claim would destroy diversity jurisdiction.

4.3.0.3 Common Nucleus of Operative Fact: *United Mine Workers of Am. v. Gibbs*

Federal courts can exercise supplemental [pendent] jurisdiction if the claims arise from a "common nucleus of operative fact."

1. Facts:

    (a) Spring 1960: The Tennessee Consolidated Coal company laid off 100 miners belonging to the United Mine Workers Local 5881.

    (b) Summer 1960: Grundy Company, a subsidiary of Consolidated, hired Gibbs to serve as superintendent for the opening of a new mine that would employ members of the Southern Labor Union. Grundy also awarded him a contract to haul the mine's coal to the railroad.

    (c) August 15, 1960: UMW Local 5881 workers forcibly prevented the opening of the new mine, believing that Consolidated had offered them the jobs, not SLU. Gibbs lost his job as superintendent and was unable to perform his hauling contract.

2. Gibbs sued UMW in district court under the Labor Management Relations Act, which established federal question jurisdiction. He also made a state law claim for interference with his employment and hauling contracts.

3. The district court rejected the LMRA claim and the hauling contract claim, but it awarded damages for Gibbs for the employment interference claim.

4. The key question before the Supreme Court was whether the district court "properly entertained" jurisdiction of the state law claim.[39]

5. The Court held that federal courts can exercise supplemental [then, pendent] jurisdiction over state law claims if they arise from a "common nucleus of operative fact" with a federal claim.[40]

4.3.0.4 Supplemental Jurisdiction and Third-Party Defendants: *Owen Equip. & Erection Co. v. Kroger*

There is no supplemental jurisdiction for plaintiffs' claims against third-party defendants if the claim would destroy diversity jurisdiction.

1. James Kroger was electrocuted when the crane he was walking next to came too close to a power line.

2. Mrs. Kroger (Iowa) brought suit in district court in Nebraska against the Omaha Public Power District (Nebraska) for negligence based on diversity jurisdiction. OPPD impleaded Owen under FRCP 14(a) as a third-party defendant. Kroger amended her complaint to assert a new claim against Owen directly. OPPD left the case when the court granted its motion for summary judgment, leaving only Kroger's direct claim against Owen.

3. On the third day of the trial, Owen revealed it was also from Iowa, eliminating diversity jurisdiction. It moved to dismiss for lack of jurisdiction. The district court denied the motion and the jury found for Kroger. The Eight Circuit affirmed.

4. Justice Stewart: Kroger's claim against Owen was independent from its claim against OPPD, even though they arose from a common nucleus of operative fact. Therefore, there was no supplemental jurisdiction, and there was no diversity jurisdiction because both parties were from Iowa. Reversed.

5. Justice White, dissenting: Kroger did not deliberately circumvent the diversity requirement. Efficiency considerations weigh in favor of keeping the case in federal court.

---

[39] Casebook p. 410.
[40] Casebook p. 411.

4.4 Removal

1. 28 U.S.C. § 1441 allows a defendant to remove a case from state to federal court.

2. 28 U.S.C. § 1446 describes the procedure for removal, including time limits.

3. Only defendants can remove.

4. All defendants must consent (except those joined under 28 U.S.C. § 1441(c)).

5. Only state → federal. No federal → state.

6. Removal does not expand federal subject matter jurisdiction. *Caterpillar.*

7. The defendant is the **master of her complaint.** She is free to bring her action in state court.

4.4.0.5 Removal and Subject Matter Jurisdiction: *Caterpillar Inc. v. Williams*

Removal does not establish subject matter jurisdiction.

1. The plaintiffs alleged that they entered into oral employment contracts with Caterpillar, which they claim Caterpillar violated when it closed its San Leandro plant and laid off the plaintiffs.

2. The plaintiffs sued for breach of contract in state court. Caterpillar removed to district court on the grounds that any individual employment contracts were superseded by collective bargaining agreements, for which LMRA preempted state law.

3. The district court held that removal was proper. The Ninth Circuit reversed.

4. The Supreme Court affirmed the Ninth Circuit's holding that removal was improper. It reasoned that the plaintiff's claim was based on a private contract dispute for which their was no subject matter jurisdiction in federal court. The well pleaded complaint rule prevented Caterpillar from removing to federal court solely on the basis of a federal defense.

    (a) There is significant dispute on this point. First, once the federal defense is pleaded as a basis for removal, it is no longer a hypothetical defense. Second, it might be unfair to prevent a defendant who relies on federal law to have a federal forum to determine its federal rights.

5. Affirmed.

4.5 Venue, Transfer, and *Forum Non Conveniens*

1. Broadly, venue tells you which district you can sue in.

2. Venue refers "to the **geographic specification of the proper court or courts** for the litigation of a civil action that is within the subject matter jurisdiction of the district courts in general." 28 U.S.C. § 1390(a). I.e., which court *within the proper system* can a plaintiff bring a case?

3. **The primary purpose of venue is to protect the defendant.**[41]

4. 28 U.S.C. § 1391, **"Venue generally"**: determines the federal district where a defendant can be sued. **Venue cannot create personal jurisdiction where none otherwise exists.** It can only *narrow*, not expand.

5. 28 U.S.C. § 1404, **"Change of venue"**: determines when and how a case can be transferred between federal districts—"for convenience . . . in the interest of justice . . . " Federal courts cannot transfer to state courts.

6. 28 U.S.C. § 1406: **"Cure of waiver of defects"**: how to deal with improper venue.

7. Most venue requirements are waivable.

8. In 2011, Congress abolished the distinction between "local" and "transitory" actions.[42]

9. **Transfer of venue**: state → state or federal → federal. Removal: state → federal.

10. *Forum non conveniens* asks whether the there's a more convenient forum where the case should be adjudicated. *Piper*.

11. Successful *forum non conveniens* motions result in dismissal.

12. Differences in substantive law are insufficient to dismiss under *forum non conveniens* unless the law in the target forum is egregiously bad. *Piper*.

4.5.1 *Forum Non Conveniens* and Differences in Substantive Law: *Piper Aircraft Co. v. Reyno*

Differences in substantive law are insufficient to dismiss under *forum non conveniens* unless the law in the target forum is egregiously bad.

1. Six people were killed when a small plane crashed in Scotland. On behalf of the decedents, the plaintiff sued the aircraft manufacturer (Piper) and the propeller manufacturer (Hartzell) in a California superior court.

---

[41] Casebook p. 449.
[42] Supplement p. 50.

2. Piper successfully removed to federal court in California under § 1441(a), relying on diversity jurisdiction (§ 1332(a)(2), (c)(2)). It then moved for transfer to the Middle District Court of Pennsylvania under 28 U.S.C. 1404(a) (change of venue for convenience). Then, in district court, it moved to dismiss on the grounds of *forum non conveniens* because it wanted to try the case in Scotland. The district court granted the motion, and the defendants agreed to submit to the jurisdiction of Scottish courts. The court noted several private interest and public policy reasons for moving the venue to Scotland.[43]

3. The Third Circuit reversed the motion to dismiss, arguing (1) that the district court did not have the authority to review the policy reasons for dismissal and (2) that dismissal is never appropriate when the law of the alternative forum is less favorable to the plaintiff.

4. The Supreme Court rejected the Third Circuit on both questions:

   (a) Differences in substantive law between two forums should never be a substantial factor unless the alternative forum is egregiously bad.

   (b) It held that the district court did not abuse its discretion in weighing the public and private interests, on the basis that foreign plaintiffs deserve less deference in determining the convenience of a forum.

---

[43]Casebook p. 474–75.

§ 5 The Governing Law in the Federal Courts

1. Holmes: "The common law is not a brooding omnipresence in the sky, but the articulate voice of some sovereign or quasi sovereign that can be identified . . . "[44]

2. **"Rules of Decision Act"** determines which law applies in federal courts: "The laws of the several states, except where the Constitution or treaties of the United States or Acts of Congress otherwise require or provide, shall be regarded as rules of decision in civil actions in the courts of the United States, in cases where they apply.[45]

3. The **Rules Enabling Act** (28 U.S.C. § 2071–2077) gives the federal court system the power to adopt federal rules. The act stipulates that procedural rules **"shall not abridge, enlarge or modify any substantive right."** § 2072.

4. The Supreme Court's interpretation of the Rules of Decision Act differed sharply betwen *Swift* (the old rule) and *Erie* (the new rule). Previously, federal courts applied **general federal common law**. After *Erie*, federal courts apply the law that the highest court in the state would apply.[46]

5. If disregarding state law would significantly affect the outcome of the case, the **outcome determinative test** requires the court to apply state law. *York*. However, the Court scaled back the test in *Byrd*, where it held that strong federal interests can weigh in favor of applying state law.

6. In *Hanna*, the Court held that courts should apply federal *procedural* rules if they conflict with state rules. (The *Erie* doctrine still applies to *substantive* law.) The Court developed a two-part test to determine whether to apply state or federal procedural law. See below for the full test.

7. A federal procedural rule displaces a state rule *only if* there is an unavoidable conflict between the two. *Walker*.

8. Federal substantive common law still applies in some limited circumstances. *Clearfield Trust*.

5.1 General Law over State Law: *Swift v. Tyson*

Where state law deviates from general law, federal courts should follow general federal common law, *not* state common law.

---

[44] *Southern Pac. Co. v. Jensen* 244 U.S. 205, 222 (1917).

[45] 28 U.S.C. § 1652, originally codified in civil § 34 of the Judicial Act of 1789. See Casebook p. 489.

[46] This is often the law of the state in which the court sits. Often, though, other factors require application of another state's law, such as in *Erie*, where the New York federal court applied Pennsylvania state law.

1. Swift owned a bill of exchange that Tyson originally made to two other men, who endorsed it over to Swift. Tyson refused to pay because of a breach of the original contract for which the bill of exchange was originally issued.

2. Swift sued Tyson in federal court for payment. Under "local" law (New York state law), which the state court followed, Tyson's defense was valid. Under "general" law, which federal courts followed, the defense was not valid against Swift.

3. § 34 of the Judiciary Act of 1789 required the application of "the laws of the several states...in cases where they apply" unless federal law otherwise required (roughly equivalent to 28 U.S.C. §1652).

4. In a unanimous opinion, Justice Story held that the federal court "should follow the general law rather than a state's local law in cases where the state law deviated from the general law."[47]

5. After the Civil War, the economic interests of the states began to diverge (north: finance, manufacturing; south: agriculture, labor). The Supreme Court expanded general law to include torts, so industrial accidents were increasingly litigated in federal courts. Federal courts also grew increasingly sympathetic to creditors and employers. Those who favored the results of state courts became enemies of *Swift*.

5.2 No Federal General Common Law: *Erie R.R. Co. v. Tompkins*

"Except in matters governed by the Federal Constitution or by acts of Congress, the law to be applied in any case is the law of the state . . . . **There is no federal general common law.**"[48]

1. A passing train injured Tompkins was while he was walking on a footpath along a railroad track in Pennsylvania. He brought suit against the Erie Railroad Co. in federal court in New York.[49]

---

[47]Casebook p. 491.
[48]Casebook p. 497.
[49]Prof. Bradt, 10/2/12: "One note clarifying something at the end of our discussion today. I believe that Mr. Mornin wanted to know why Harry Tompkins wanted to filed his case in federal court in New York as opposed to federal court in Pennsylvania.

He could have filed in federal court in either state (based on diversity), there was likely personal jurisdiction over the Erie in Pennsylvania (even under 1930s-era personal-jurisdiction doctrine, the Erie would have been considered to be "doing business" in Pennsylvania, at least when it came to an accident in Pennsylvania), and venue would have been fine, too (in those days, venue could be based on the residence of the plaintiff).

The decision to file in federal vs. state court is clear: Tompkins wanted the benefit of federal general common law, as opposed to PA state law, which was terrible for him. But why NY federal court as opposed to PA federal court?

Well, the answer lies in the lack of uniformity of general federal common law. Not only did *Swift* not achieve uniformity between federal and state courts on issues of tort law, it

2. Under Pennsylvania state law, Tompkins would have been considered a trespasser and therefore not entitled to recover damages. Under general law, the railroad might have been held negligent.

3. The legal circumstances were unusual. At the time, "general law" usually benefited corporations, while "local law" usually favored individuals. In this case, however, the plaintiff argued for the application of general law.

4. The trial court and appellate court, following *Swift*, found that since no state statute governed the issue at hand, general law should control. They found for the plaintiff. The issue before the Supreme Court was whether the district court was free to disregard Pennsylvania common law.

5. Justice Brandeis:

    (a) The *Swift* court had misinterpreted the intentions of the authors of the Judiciary Act of 1789: " . . . the construction given to it by the court was erroneous; and that the purpose of the section was merely to make certain that, in all matters except those in which some federal law is controlling, the federal courts exercising jurisdiction in diversity of citizenship cases would apply as their rules of decision the law of the state, unwritten as well as written."[50] (The notes point out that the historian on whom the opinion relies, Charles Warren, might have mistakenly interpreted the Rules of Decision Act as requiring federal courts to follow state common law even in areas where federal common law applied.)

    (b) *Swift* caused significant "injustice and confusion"[51]—e.g., companies reincorporating in other states in order to establish diversity jurisdiction to have their cases tried in federal court (*Black & White Taxicab*). "*Swift v. Tyson* introduced grave discrimination by noncitizens against citizens."[52]

    (c) The federal government did not have the power to legislate rules of tort or contract law.[53] Federal courts also do not have the power to create rules in these areas.

    (d) Reversed and remanded to be decided on the basis of Pennsylvania state law.

---

also did not achieve uniformity *among* federal courts. A federal court sitting in Pennsylvania (governed by the law of the Third Circuit) would have applied more defense-friendly law than the federal court sitting in New York (governed by the Second Circuit). It's possible, in fact, that the PA federal district court would have deferred to PA law in Tompkins's case because the Third Circuit's view of *Swift* was a little less expansive than the Second Circuit's. So even though general federal common law would have applied in federal court sitting in PA and NY, the NY federal court would have been a friendlier forum."

[50] Casebook p. 495.
[51] Casebook p. 501.
[52] Casebook p. 496.
[53] This quickly became untrue as the Court expanded the federal government's power to regulate these areas under the Commerce Clause.

5 THE GOVERNING LAW IN THE FEDERAL COURTS

(e) The *Swift* rule is overturned.

6. "Except in matters governed by the Federal Constitution or by acts of Congress, the law to be applied in any case is the law of the state .... There is no federal general common law."[54] Judges often relied on "general law" as a way of ignoring state laws that conflicted with their views.

7. Justice Reed, concurring:

    (a) It is enough to broaden the *Swift* framework to hold that "the laws" in the Rules of Decison Act include state common law, rather than declare the entire *Swift framework* to be unconstitutional.

    (b) It's "questionable" to say that Congress has no power to declare which substantive laws control in federal courts—moreso because "[t]he line between procedural and substantive law is hazy."[55]

5.3 "Outcome Determinative" Test: *Guaranty Trust v. York*

The **"outcome determinative" test**: would it significantly affect the outcome of the litigation for a federal court to disregard state law? If so, *Erie* holds that the court should follow state law.

1. Background:

    (a) **Substance vs. procedure**: did *Erie* and the Rules of Decision Act apply to both procedural and substantive law?

    (b) Before the FRCP were enacted in 1938, courts were divided into courts of law (in which cases were triable by jury) and courts of equity (where there was no right to a jury).

    (c) The **Conformity Act of 1872** required that in cases *at law*, federal courts must conform to the procedural rules of the states in which they were located. Thus, there were procedural differences between federal courts in different states, but few differences between federal and state courts in the same state. In cases *in equity*, federal and state courts followed different rules. Federal courts developed their own system of procedural rules for suits brought in equity.[56]

    (d) The **Rules Enabling Act of 1934** authorized the Supreme Court (with congressional approval) to develop, with the consent of Congress, a national system of procedural rules for federal civil cases. So while *Erie* required federal courts to follow state rules in substantive law, federal courts developed independent procedural rules (codified in the FRCP in 1938).

---

[54]Casebook p. 497.
[55]Casebook p. 499.
[56]Casebook p. 504.

2. York brought suit in 1942 equity in New York federal court for fraud that occurred in 1931. The defendants argued that the New York statute of limitations applied to cases both at law and in equity. The plaintiff argued that the federal rule of laches, which typically applied in equity cases, should apply in this case.

3. The trial court agreed with the plaintiff and applied the New York statute of limitations. The appellate court reversed, holding that the federal laches doctrine should have applied, and granted summary judgment to the defendants.

4. Justice Frankfurter:

   (a) There is not a clear distinction between "substantive" and "procedural" rights.

   (b) This case dealt with a state-created right. When a federal court adjudicates a state-created right solely on the basis of jurisdiction, it becomes "in effect, only another court of the State."

   (c) Does the statute of limitations affect "merely the manner and the means" of the right to recover, or is it "a matter of substance" that affects the result of the litigation?

   (d) *Erie* did not intend to "formulate scientific legal terminology" around the terms "substantive" and "procedural." It intended to ensure that outcomes of diversity cases in federal court would be similar to outcomes in state courts. If outcomes were different, we're back to the discriminatory days of *Swift*.

   (e) The *Erie* doctrine does not distinguish between cases at law and cases in equity.

   (f) "The source of substantive rights enforced by a federal court under diversity jurisdiction, it cannot be said too often, is the law of the States. Whenever that law is authoritatively declared by a State, whether its voice be the legislature or its highest court, such law ought to govern in litigation founded on that law, whether the forum of application is a State or a federal court and whether the remedies be sought at law or may be had in equity."[57]

   (g) Reversed and remanded for hearings consistent with the New York statute of limitations.

5. Justice Rutledge, dissenting:

   (a) The distinction between "substantive" and "procedural" law is arbitrary but important.

   (b) Forum states are free to apply their own statutes of limitations, which may be different from those of the state that originally created the substantive right.

---

[57]Casebook p. 507.

5.4 Really Regulating Procedure: *Sibbach v. Wilson & Co.*

According to the Rules Enabling Act, the federal rules "shall neither abridge, enlarge, nor modify the substantive rights of any litigant." A rule is procedural if it "really regulates procedure."

1. A federal court required the plaintiff to submit to a mandatory medical examination. The examination would not have been mandatory under Illinois state law. She refused the exam on the grounds that the Rules Enabling Act forbade rules that abridge litigants' substantive rights. The court held "[t]he test must be whether a rule **really regulates procedure.**"[58]

2. Justice Frankfurter (and three others) dissented, arguing that the examination rule constituted "invasion of the person" and was therefore significantly different from other procedural rules.

5.5 "Byrd Balancing": *Byrd v. Blue Ridge Rural Elec. Coop.*

Byrd balancing: even if a state rule is outcome determinative, countervailing federal considerations can tip the balance in favor of applying federal rules.

1. Byrd sued the defendant in North Carolina district court for negligence for an injury he sustained while connecting power lines.

2. The defendant argued that the plaintiff was a "statutory employee" under the South Carolina Workmen's Compensation Act when the injury occurred, which would mean that the plaintiff was barred from suing and was obliged to accept statutory compensation benefits.

3. The district court found for Byrd. The Fourth Circuit reversed.

4. The questions before the Supreme Court were (1) whether the appellate court erred in directing judgment for Blue Ridge without giving Byrd an opportunity to introduce further evidence, and (2) whether Byrd is entitled to a jury to determine factual issues.

5. Justice Brennan:

    (a) Blue Ridge argued that a judge, not a jury, should decide the question of immunity. In *Adams v. Davidson-Paxon Co.*, the South Carolina Supreme court held that a judge, not a jury, should determine the question of whether the plaintiff was a statutory employee (and therefore whether the employer is immune from paying damages). The defendant's argument contends that the federal court should follow this state precedent.

---

[58] Casebook p. 509.

(b) *Erie* held that in diversity cases, federal courts must respect state-created rights by state courts. Here, the Supreme Court found that the decision in *Adams* to send the immunity question to a judge was a "practical consideration"—"merely a form and mode"—"and not a rule intended to be bound up with the definition of the rights and obligations of the parties."

(c) Mere "form and mode" rules can be important if they bear substantially on the outcome of the litigation (cf. *York*). It may be in this case that the question of whether immunity should be decided by a judge or jury would bear substantially on the outcome. Here, however, there is a general federal policy of sending factual questions to the jury. Even though it may affect the outcome, the federal rule should outweigh the state rule because a federal procedural rule is "not in any sense a local matter."

(d) Third, it is not at all clear that sending the immunity question to a jury would result in a different outcome.

(e) The federal rule applies. Reversed and remanded.

5.6 State vs. Federal Procedural Rules: *Hanna v. Plumer*

The "*Hanna* holding" and "*Hanna* dictum" tests determine when the court should follow state or federal procedural rules.

1. Hanna was involved in an auto accident in South Carolina. He sued the executor of the other driver's estate, Plumer, in Massachusetts district court.

2. In accord with the Federal Rules, Hanna served process by leaving copies of the summons with the defendant's wife at their residence. Plumer argued that the conflicting Massachusetts statute requiring service in person should apply. If the Massachusetts standard applied, the statute of limitations would have run.

3. The district court granted summary judgment for Plumer and the First Circuit affirmed.

4. Justice Warren developed a two-prong test for federal procedural rules:[59]

---

[59]The Supreme Court offered a slightly different framing of the *Hanna* test in *Burke v. Smith*: " . . . the Supreme Court developed a two-part test in *Hanna v. Plumer* . . . . Under the *Hanna* test, 'when the federal law sought to be applied is a congressional statute or Federal Rule of Civil Procedure, the district court must first decide whether the statute is 'sufficiently broad to control the issue before the court." . . . If the federal procedural rule is 'sufficiently broad to control the issue' and conflicts with the state law, the federal procedural rule applies instead of the state law . . . . If the federal rule does not directly conflict with the state law, then the second prong of the *Hanna* test requires the district court to evaluate 'whether failure to apply the state law would lead to different outcomes in state and federal court and result in inequitable administration of the laws or forum shopping.'"

(a) What is the source of the procedural rule?
  i. Congressional rule, i.e., FRCP or statute ("*Hanna* holding"):
    - Is the federal rule **pertinent**? I.e., is there an unavoidable conflict with a state procedural rule? If no, apply the federal rule. If yes:
    - Is the federal rule **valid**?[60]
      – Is it **constitutional**? I.e., is it "rationally capable of classification as procedural?"
      – Is it consistent with the **Rules Enabling Act**? I.e., does it "really regulate procedure" (*Sibbach*) without abridging substantive rights?
    - → If the rule is invalid, apply the state rule. Otherwise, apply the federal rule.
  i. Judge-made rule ("*Hanna* dictum"):
    - Is the difference between the state and federal rules **outcome determinative**? If not, apply the federal rule. If yes:
    - Does the difference implicate the twin aims of *Erie?*
      A. Does the difference encourage **forum shopping**?
      B. Does the difference cause **inequitable administration of the law**. Can you explain to your client why being in federal vs. state court makes a difference?
      C. If the difference *does* implicate both the twin aims, apply the state rule. Otherwise, apply the federal rule.

5. Applying the test, the court found that (1) the rule in question was congressional, (2) it unavoidably conflicted with the Massachusetts rule, (3) it was constitutional, and (4) it was consistent with the Rules Enabling Act. Thus, the federal rule applied.

6. Reversed.

5.7 Applying the *Hanna* Test: *Walker v. Armco Steel Corp.*

Under the *Hanna* test, a federal procedural rule displaces a state rule only if there is an unavoidable conflict between the two.

1. A nail head fragmented and injured Walker's eye. He sued the manufacturer, Armco, in Oklahoma district court.

2. The district court dismissed the action on the grounds that under Oklahoma procedural rules, the statute of limitations (two years) and the service period (60 days) had run. The Tenth Circuit affirmed.

---

[60] No FRCP has ever been found to be invalid, thought the Court has interpreted them narrowly to preserve their validity.

3. On appeal, Walker argued that the court should follow FRCP 3, which states only that a civil action commences when the plaintiff files a complaint with a court.

4. Justice Marshall:

    (a) Walker argued that there is a direct conflict between the state and federal procedural rules. Under *Hanna*, this would mean that the federal rule prevails.

    (b) In this case, however, there was no unavoidable conflict between the state and federal rules. "There is no indication that the [federal] Rule was intended to toll a state statute of limitations," much less displace state rules.[61]

    (c) State law should have applied. Under the Oklahoma rule, the statute of limitations had run. Affirmed.

5.8 Standards of Appellate Review: *Gasperini v. Center for Humanities*

State statutes regarding the standard of review for excessive jury verdicts are substantive, not procedural, and federal courts are therefore obligated to follow them.

1. The Center for Humanities lost 300 of Gasperini's slides. He sued in New York district court. The trial court awarded $450,000 in compensatory damages.

2. A New York statute required reversal of an "excessive" jury award if it "deviates materially from what would be reasonable compensation."

3. Justice Ginsburg: the New York statute was a "manifestly substantive" policy. The federal court must apply the state standard. Remanded for a new trial so that the judge could apply the state standard to the jury's verdict.

5.9 Federal Common Law: *Clearfield Trust Co v. United States*

Although there is no general federal common law, courts can still apply federal common law in particular circumstances.

1. A paycheck to Clair Barner from the WPA was stolen, Barner's signature forged, and cashed by Clearfield Trust at a JC Penney.

---

[61] 446 U.S. 740 (1980).

2. The government sued Clearfield Trust in Pennsylvania district court. The court determined that Pennsylvania state law controlled, and therefore dismissed the complaint because the government was too slow to notify Clearfield of the forgery.

3. The Third Circuit reversed.

4. Justice Douglas: the government's interest in uniformity and certainty in its financial dealings weighed in favor of applying federal law over state law. "The issuance of commercial paper by the United States is on a vast scale and transactions in that paper from issuance to payment will commonly occur in several states. The application of state law, even without the conflict of laws rules of the forum, would subject the rights and duties of the United States to exceptional uncertainty. It would lead to great diversity in results by making identical transactions subject to the vagaries of the laws of the several states. The desirability of a uniform rule is plain." Affirmed.

§ 6 Pleading

1. Four parts:

    (a) **Parties**: who are we?

    (b) **PJ, SMJ, Venue**: how are we here?

    (c) **Subject of the case**: why are we here?

    (d) **Remedy sought**: what do we want?

2. FRCP 8 guides the **substance** of pleadings, requiring (a) a plaintiff's pleading to contain a statement of jurisdiction, a statement of the claim, a demand for relief, and (b) a response to include a defense to each claim, admission or denial of each allegation (or a general denial).

3. FRCP 10 guides the **form** of pleadings.

4. **Motion to dismiss for failure to state a claim** (12)(b)(6):

    (a) Defendant makes the motion.

    (b) Accept the allegations as true.

    (c) View the evidence in the light most favorable to the plaintiff.

    (d) Deny unless "clear that no relief could be granted under any set of facts that could be proved consistent with the complaint." *Swierkiewicz*.

    (e) Liberal policy of leave to amend in response to a 12(b)(6) motion.

5. Original pleading requirements were liberal: **"short and plain statement"**. 8(a).

6. Balance of policies: access to court; adjudication on the merits; prevent hopeless litigation under 12(b)(6) but keep it in if there's doubt.

7. *Conley*: do not grant 12(b)(6) "unless it appears beyond doubt that the plaintiff can prove no set of facts in support of his claim which would entitle him to relief."

8. In *Swierkiewicz*, the court interpreted the pleading requirements under FRCP 8 to be loose and liberal. The pleader need only state a legally cognizable claim. There is no requirement to produce evidence.

9. Before *Twombly*, a pleading was sufficient if it was **conceivable**. Now, a claim must be **plausible**. The full *Twombly* standard:

    (a) Pleading must contain a short and plain statement (Rule 8).

    (b) The court accepts facts as true.

    (c) The court draws all reasonable inferences in favor of the plaintiff.

6 PLEADING

(d) The court determines whether the complain is *plausible on its face*, meaning it must be more than a mere possibility and not merely consistent with the defendant's liability.

(e) Plaintiffs must "nudge[] their claims across the line from conceivable to plausible."

10. **Pleading in the alternative** allows multiple inconsistent claims. Throw spaghetti against the wall and see what sticks. *McCormick*.

11. Misconduct is sanctionable under **Rule 11**. *Zuk*.

12. FRCP 8(b) requires responses to claims to explicitly affirm or deny each element of a claim. *Zielinski*.

13. Complaints can be **amended** before and during the trial under the conditions of Rule 15.

14. **Rule 11** governs duties and sanctions in pleading.

    (a) **Duties** (11(b)): reasonable investigation into the client's claims; suit is not for improper purpose; legal contention are not frivolous; factual contentions have actual or likely evidentiary support; denials are warranted based on lack of evidence, belief of lack of evidence, or lack of information.

    (b) **Enforcement** (11(c)): parties can move for sanctions or the court can sanction on its own.

6.1 FRCP 8: General Rules of Pleading

- (a) Pleading must contain:
    - (1) Short and plain statement of jurisdiction.
    - (2) Short and plain statement of claim.
    - (3) Demand for relief.
- (b) Defenses; Admissions and Denials:
    - (1) General response:
        * (A) Short and plain statement of defense to each claim.
        * (B) Admit or deny allegations.
    - (2) Denial must respond to substance of allegation.
    - (3) General denial will deny everything. Otherwise, specific allegations must be separately admitted or denied.
    - (4) Denial in part requires admission of the part that's true and denial of the rest.
    - (5) Defense must acknowledge lack of knowledge where it exists, which has the effect of a denial.
    - (6) Failure to deny = admission.

6.2 FRCP 10: Form of Pleadings

- (a) Caption/names of parties.

- (b) Paragraphs must be numbered; independent statements must be separated.

- (c) Adoption by reference.

6.3 Liberal Pleading Requirements: *Swierkiewicz v. Sorema, N.A.*

Complaints need not contain evidentiary details. They "must contain only 'a short and plain statement of the claim showing that the pleader is entitled to relief.'"

1. Swiekiewicz alleged employment discrimination based on his age and nationality.

2. The Southern District of New York dismissed for having "not alleged a prima facie case, in that he had not alleged circumstances supporting an inference of discrimination."[62] The Second Circuit affirmed.

3. Justice Thomas:

    (a) The lower courts' reliance on *McDonnell Douglas* was misplaced because that case established an evidentiary requirement, not a *pleading* requirement.

    (b) Rule 8's simple standard should apply here. In *Conley*, the Court held that "The Federal Rules reject the approach that pleading is a game of skill."[63]

    (c) Reversed.

6.4 Plausible Pleadings: *Bell Atlantic v. Twombly*

Plaintiffs must state a plausible claim, not merely a conceivable one.

1. The plaintiffs alleged that ILECs inflated charges for local phone and high-speed Internet service by (1) engaging in "parallel conduct" to inhibit startup CLECs and (2) agreeing not to compete with each other. The plaintiffs provided little factual basis for their claims.

2. The Southern District of New York dismissed for failure to state a claim. The Second Circuit reversed.

3. Justice Souter:

---

[62] Casebook p. 609.
[63] Casebook p. 612.

6 PLEADING

(a) In complaints, "[f]actual allegations must be enough to raise a right to relief *above the speculative level.*" The complaint needs "enough fact to raise a reasonable expectation that discovery will reveal evidence of illegal agreement."[64]

(b) Discovery can be expensive, and in this case, especially expensive.

(c) Reversed.

6.5 Affirming *Twombly*: *Ashcroft v. Iqbal*

1. Iqbal was detained after 9/11. His complaint against Ashcroft and Mueller alleged unconstitutionally harsh confinement on account of his race, religion, or national origin.

2. The district court denied Ashcroft's motion to dismiss for failure to state a claim. The Second Circuit affirmed.

3. Justice Kennedy:

    (a) After *Twombly*, Rule 8(a)(2) requires "further factual enhancement."

    (b) The claim must be plausible. Iqbal's was not. Reversed.

6.6 Pleading in the Alternative: *McCormick v. Kopmann*

Parties can plead claims that are fundamentally inconsistent. Pleadings are not binding admissions. They're hypotheses subject to proof and disproof.

1. McCormick, the widow of a man killed in a collision with Kopmann, made two claims that were at issue on appeal:

    (a) Count I: wrongful death against Kopmann.

    (b) Count IV: dram shop claim against the Huls.

2. The defendants moved for directed verdicts. Denied. The jury returned a verdict for $15,000 against Kopmann and found the Huls not guilty. Kopmann moved for judgment notwithstanding the verdict or for a new trial; both were denied.

3. Kopmann appealed, arguing:

    (a) Counts I and IV were mutually exclusive. The court agreed, but held that this does not prevent them from being pleaded together. The Illinois Civil Practice Act (modeled on FRCP 8(e)(2), which allows alternative pleading where the plaintiff is "genuinely in doubt as to what the facts are and what the evidence will show"[65]).

---

[64] Casebook p. 620.
[65] Caseboko p. 663.

(b) Allegations of intoxication in Count IV count as binding admissions. Court held that "he is not 'admitting' anything other than his uncertainty."[66]

(c) Prima facie case in Count IV means plaintiff was contributorily negligent regarding count one. The court found that the plaintiff did exercise due care and was not intoxicated.

4. Affirmed.

6.7 Sanctions: *Zuk v. E. Penn. Psychiatric Institute*

Misconduct is sanctionable under Rule 11.

1. Zuk sued EPPI for copyright infringement. The district court dismissed under FRCP 12(b)(6) (motion to dismiss) and found Zuk and his counsel liable for $15,000 in sanctions and counsel fees. Zuk settled his liability. His counsel, Lipman, appealed.

2. EPPI moved for sanctions "on the grounds essentially that appellant had failed to conduct an inquiry into the facts reasonable under the circumstances and into the law."[67] The court imposed sanctions based on FRCP 11 and 28 U.S.C.§ 1927.

3. The Third Circuit held:

    (a) Lipman had no liability under the Copyright Act.

    (b) There was no bad faith on Lipman's part. Therefore, the lower court abused its discretion in awarding sanctions based on 28 U.S.C. § 1927.

    (c) The lower court did not identify exactly how the sanctions were based on the FRCP and USC rules. The FRCP sanctions were appropriate, because the original plaintiffs' research was deficient both factually and legally, but it is not possible to review them further. Remanded to consider the type and amount of sanctions specific to the FRCP violation.

    (d) " . . . we conclude that it was in error to invoke without comment a very severe penalty."[68]

6.8 FRCP 11: Signing, Representations, Sanctions

- (a) Attorney (or self-represented party) must sign all papers.

- (b) Representations must:

    – (1) Not have any improper purpose.

---

[66]Casebook p. 664.
[67]Casebook p. 671.
[68]Casebook p. 678.

6 PLEADING

- (2) Make claims warranted by law or make nonfrivolous arguments for changing the law.
- (3) Have evidentiary support (or probably support) for factual contentions.
- (4) Make denials of factual contentions warranted by evidence, reasonable belief, or lack of information.

- (c) Sanctions:
  - (1) After notice and opportunity to be heard, court may sanction an attorney, firm, or party for 11(b) violations. Law firms must be held jointly responsible.
  - (2) Motions for sanctions must be made separately. The party has 21 days from the date of service to withdraw the challenged paper. The court can award expenses to the prevailing party.
  - (3) On its own initiative, a court can ask a party to show why it hasn't violated 11(b).
  - (4) Sanctions must be limited to what is necessary for deterrence. Sanctions can be nonmonetary or monetary.
  - (5) Limits on monetary sanctions:
    * Courts cannot sanction a represented party for violating 11(b)(2) (i.e., lawyers are responsible for legal contentions).
    * Courts cannot impose monetary sanctions unless it issues an 11(c)(3) show-cause order before dismissal or settlement.
  - (6) A sanction order must include an explanation.
- (d) Rule 11 does not apply to discovery motions.

6.9 FRCP 12: Defenses and Objections

6.10 Explicit Affirmation or Denial: *Zielinski v. Philadelphia Piers*

FRCP 8(b) requires responses to claims to explicitly affirm or deny each element of a claim.

1. Facts:
   (a) February 9, 1953: Sandy Johnson crashed a forklift into Frank Zielinski, causing injuries.
   (b) February 10, 1953: Carload Contractors, Inc. sent an accident report to its insurance company.
   (c) April 28, 1953: Zielinski filed complaint against Philadelphia Piers, Inc., arguing that (1) PPI owned the forklift that Johnson was operating and (2) Johnson was acting as an employee of PPI.

6 PLEADING

(d) April 29, 1953: complaint was forwarded to the insurance company.

(e) June 12, 1953: PPI's general manager responded to interrogatories 1 through 5.

(f) August 19, 1953: Sandy Johnson testified in a deposition that he was an employee of PPI.

(g) September 27, 1955: Pre-trial conference held where Zielinski learned that the work of moving freight on the piers had been sold to Carload Contractors, Inc., and that Johnson became an employee of Carload.

(h) October 21, 1955: From the answers to supplementary interrogatories, plaintiff learned that the accident report had been submitted to the insurance company.

2. The district court held:

(a) In the original complaint, Zielinski claimed that PPI owned the forklift and that Johnson was an employee of PPI. Initially, PPI simply responded, "Defendant ... denies the averments of paragraph 5."[69]

(b) PPI's response was inadequate. It meant to only deny the claim of employee negligence, but it should have also addressed the question of whether PPI owned and operated the forklift. PPI's response led Zielinski to believe that PPI was the owner and operator of the forklift, but in fact it had been sold to CCI. Zielinski sued the wrong company, but by the time he learned his mistake (September 27, 1955), the statute of limitations had run.

(c) FRCP 8(b) requires responses to claims to explicitly affirm or deny each element of a claim.

(d) The court held that the doctrine of equitable estoppel requires that the case go forward against PPI with the record showing that PPI owned and operated the forklift—even though that wasn't actually the case.

6.11 FRCP 15: Amended and Supplemental Pleadings

- (a) Amendments before trial.
- (b) Amendments during and after trial.
- (c) Relation back of amendments.
- (d) Supplemental pleadings.

---

[69] Casebook p. 686.

6.12 Amendments Relating Back: *Worthington v. Wilson*

Complaints can be amended to name a different party as long as the new party had notice.

1. Facts:

    (a) February 25, 1989: Worthington was arrested by two police officers.

    (b) February 25, 1991: Worthington filed a complaint against the Village of Peoria Heights in county court against "three unknown named police officers." The Village removed the action to the District Court for the Central District of Illinois.

    (c) June 17, 1991: Worthington amended his complaint to identify the two police officers by name.

2. The statute of limitations was two years, which had expired when Worthington filed his amended complaint. Defendants argued that the amended complaint cannot related back to the filing date of the original complaint under FRCP 15(c).

3. In response, Worthington made three arguments:

    (a) Relation back was governed by an Illinois statute, not 15(c).

    (b) The 15(c) requirements were satisfied.

    (c) He should not be punished for omitting the officers' names in the original complaint because the Peoria Heights Police Department had withheld that information.

4. In *Schiavone v. Fortune* (1986), the Supreme Court held that parties to be brought in by amendment must receive notice of the action before the expiration of the statue of limitations period.

5. December 1, 1991: FRCP 15 was amended in direct response to *Schiavone*. The new rule allowed complaints to be amended at any time to correct misnamed defendants as long as the defendant was aware of the action within 120 days of the filing of the original complaint. Notice is no longer required.

6. Under the new version of FRCP 15(c), Worthington's amendment was acceptable.

7. Defendants also argued that 15(c) did not apply because the defect in Worthington's original complaint was due to lack of knowledge, not a "mistake." The Seventh Circuit had previously held that lack of knowledge of the proper defendant does not involve a mistake. The district court here disagreed, but out of deference agreed with defendants and granted their motion to dismiss.

§ 7 Joinder, Counterclaims, and Crossclaims

1. **Joinder of claims**: once a party has made a claim against another party, he can join any other claim to the suit. It is **never required** and the joined claim must have **independent subject matter jurisdiction**. Rule 18(a).

2. **Joinder of parties**:

    (a) **Permissive** (Rule 20): (a) **multiple plaintiffs** have the option to join together (if the claims arise from the same transaction or occurrence and the plaintiffs share a common question of law or fact) or (b) a plaintiff can name **multiple co-defendants** (under the same requirements as multiple plaintiffs: T&O and common question).

        i. Jurisdiction requirements must be independently satisfied, with the one exception that multiple plaintiffs can pool the amount of their claims to meet the amount in controversy requirement.

    (b) **Compulsory** (Rule 19):

        i. **Necessary** parties: without them, there can be no relief, or it would prejudice the absentee, or it would prejudice the current parties. Necessary parties must be joined if possible, but the suit continues if they can't.

        ii. **Indispensable** parties: same as necessary but where joinder is impossible because of jurisdictional problems. The indispensable parties must be joined if possible, and the **action must be dropped** if they can't. Rule 19(b) and *Helzberg*.

3. There are two types of **counterclaims**:

    (a) **Compulsory**: it arises from the same transaction and occurrence of the other party's claim. The party forfeits that claim if it does not assert it (unless the counterclaim would require an additional party over whom the court cannot get personal jurisdiction). Rule 13(a). *Is* within supplemental jurisdiction. *Jones v. Ford*.

    (b) **Permissive**: any counterclaim that is not compulsory. It need not be related to the same transaction or occurrence. *May be* within supplemental jurisdiction if it has a "loose factual connection" to the original events. *Jones v. Ford*.

4. Plaintiffs can counter-counter-claim (and that claim can be compulsory).

5. A **third-party defendant** can counterclaim against the original defendant or the original plaintiff (but only if the original plaintiff first made a claim against the third-party defendant). Rule 14(a).

6. **Supplemental jurisdiction** over counterclaims: for *compulsory* claims, yes (because they arise from the same transaction or occurrence); for *permissive* claims, probably not (because they are unrelated).

7. **Crossclaims** are claims between co-defendants or co-plaintiffs. Must have arisen from the same transaction or occurrence as the original action or counterclaim (13(g)). The party making the claim must request **actual relief** rather than just raise a defense. Never compulsory.

8. **Impleader** (14(a)):

    (a) A defendant can **implead** a **third-party defendant** he believes is liable to him (e.g., indemnity).

    (b) The claim must be derivative of the original claim, i.e., the third-party *plaintiff* can't claim he is not at all liable to the primary plaintiff.

    (c) Plaintiffs against whom counterclaims are made can implead those who are liable to them. Rule 14(b).

    (d) Service to the third-party defendant can be made within the **100-mile bulge** of the courthouse.

    (e) Supplemental jurisdiction applies.

    (f) Primary plaintiffs can assert claims against third-party defendants.

    (g) Third-party defendants can assert **claims of their own**, including:

        i. Counterclaims against the third-party plaintiff.

        ii. Crossclaims against other third-party defendants.

        iii. Counterclaims against the primary plaintiff if (a) it arises from the same transaction or occurrence as the plaintiff's original claim or (b) if the primary plaintiff asserted a claim directly against the third-party defendant.

        iv. Impleader claims against others not already in the suit.

    (h) If the primary claim is dismissed, the court has discretion whether to hear the third-party claims.

9. **Intervention**: parties can enter the lawsuit of their own initiative.

    (a) Intervention requires **independent subject matter jurisdiction**.

    (b) **Intervention of right** (24(a)): The court's permission is not required. The party can intervene if it:

        i. "claims an interest relating to the **property or transaction**" at issue;

        ii. disposing of the action would "impair or impede the movant's ability to protect its interest"; and

        iii. the interest is not adequately represented by the existing parties.

    (c) **Permissive intervention** (24(b)): The court has discretion on whether to allow the intervention. The party can intervene if it "has a claim or defense that shares with the main action a **common question of law or fact**."

7 JOINDER, COUNTERCLAIMS, AND CROSSCLAIMS

7.1 FRCP 18: Joinder of Claims

- (a) A party can join as many claims, counterclaims, and cross-claims as it has against another party.
- (b) A party may join two claims even though one of them is contingent on the disposition of the other.

7.2 FRCP 42: Consolidation; Separate Trials

- (a) If actions involve a "common question of law or fact":
    - (1) Join all matters at issue.
    - (2) Consolidate the actions.
    - (3) Issue other orders to avoid cost or delay.
- (b) Court can order separate trials.

7.3 FRCP 13: Counterclaim and Crossclaim

- (a) Compulsory counterclaims.
- (b) Permissive counterclaims.
- . . .

7.4 Counterclaims and Supplemental Jurisdiction: *Jones v. Ford Motor Credit Co.*

Compulsory counterclaims *are* within supplemental jurisdiction. Permissive counterclaims *may be* within supplemental jurisdiction if it has a "loose factual connection" to the original events.

1. Plaintiffs sued Ford Credit, individually and as class representatives, for racial discrimination under the Equal Credit Opportunity Act.

2. Ford asserted counterclaims (1) for the plaintiffs' unpaid car loans and (2) conditional counterclaims against any class members in default of their loans.

3. The district court held that Ford's counterclaims were not compulsory counterclaims and declined to exercise jurisdiction over the counterclaims.

4. Two types of counterclaims:
    (a) **Compulsory**: arising from same transaction or occurrence; forfeited if not raised.
    (b) **Permissive**: any claim not arising from the same transaction or occurrence.

5. Appellate court here agreed that Ford's counterclaims were permissive.

6. Compulsory counterclaims *do* establish supplemental jurisdiction.

7. Third Circuit rejected the view that independent jurisdiction is required for all permissive counterclaims.

8. Now, permissive counterclaims need only have a "loose factual connection" to the original facts—a broader requirement than the *Gibbs* CNOF test.[70]

9. The court held that (1) supplemental jurisdiction (under 28 U.S.C. 1367) may be available for permissive counterclaims and (2) the court should not exercise its discretion to not grant supplemental jurisdiction until it has ruled on the plaintiffs' motion for class certification.

7.5 Jurisdiction over Crossclaims: *Fairview Park v. Al Monzo*

Once the original claim has been dismissed, the court can maintain its jurisdiction to hear crossclaims.

1. Fairview sued Robinson Township, Al Monzo, and Maryland Casualty. Al Monzo crossclaimed against Robinson Township, and Robinson Township counterclaimed against Al Monzo.

2. Court dismissed Fairview's claim against Robinson Township on a statutory basis.

3. The court then dismissed Al Monzo's crossclaim against Fairview because of a lack of independent jurisdiction (since both were PA residents).

4. The court entered judgment for Fairview against Al Monzo.

5. On appeal, Al Monzo argued that "it could not be divested of jurisdiction by the Township's dismissal as a primary defendant."[71]

6. The appellate court relied on the principle that "jurisdiction which has once been attached is not lost by subsequent events."

7. Since the claim against Robinson was dismissed *not on jusridictional grounds*, Al Monzo's crossclaim can remain.

---

[70] Casebook p. 718.
[71] Casebook p. 725

7.6 Parties and Standing

1. Standing means a party has a claim that can survive a motion to dismiss.

2. Standing requirements stem from the "case or controversy" requirement of Article III.

3. Rules have been criticized as obscure and complex.

4. State courts generally follow different and simpler standing rules.

7.7 Series of Transactions or Occurrences: *Kedra v. City of Philadelphia*

An extended series of events can meet the Rule 20(a) requirement of "the same transaction, occurrence, or series of transactions or occurrences."

1. The plaintiffs brought action under the Civil Rights Act and the Constitution against city of Philadelphia and multiple police officers and officials for brutality, etc.

2. The defendants first contested the mother's prosecution of the case on behalf of her minor sons. The court rejected this as frivolous.

3. Second, the defendants second that there was an improper joinder of defendant parties because the events, which occurred over fourteen or fifteen months, did not arise from the same transaction, occurrence, or series of transactions or occurrences.

4. The court found that the events *did* arise from the same occurrences, so joinder was proper under FRCP 20(a).

5. There was also the question of whether joinder of defendants would prejudice some of them. Court held that it would be better to address this question after discovery.

7.8 Permissive and Necessary Parties: *Temple v. Synthes Corp.*

Parties who are jointly and severally liable for a tort are permissive but not compulsory for the purposes of joinder of parties.

1. Temple sued Synthes in district court and the doctor in state court. The district court ordered Temple under FRCP 19 to join the doctor or face dismissal. The appellate court agreed.

2. Here, the Supreme Court reversed because the doctor and Synthes were jointly and severally liable, which historically are *permissive* parties but not *necessary* parties.

7.9 Necessary vs. Indispensable Parties: *Helzberg's Diamond Shops v. Valley West Des Moines Shopping Center*

Joinder of a party is not compulsory if the absence of that party would not prejudice any of the current parties or the absentee.

1. Helzberg's lease with Valley West stipulated that no more than two other full jewelry shops could open in the mall. When the mall signed a lease with a fourth jewelry shop, Lord's, Helzberg sought injunctive relief against Valley West.

2. Valley West moved to dismiss because Helzberg had failed to join Lord's under FRCP 19. Denied.

3. It was not feasible for Lord's to be joined because Lord's was not subject to the court's personal jurisdiction. Under Rule 19, the court was then required to determine whether Lord's was indispensable. It decided that it was not, because Lord's absence would not prejudice it because all of its rights under its lease are maintained.

4. "In sum, it is generally recognized that a person does not become indispensable to an action to determine rights under a contract simply because that person's rights or obligations under an entirely separate contract will be affected by the result of the action."[72]

7.10 FRCP 14(a)–(b): Third-Party Practice

- (a) When a Defending Party May Bring in a Third Party.
    - (1) A defending party may bring in a third party, at which point the defending partybecomes a "third-party plaintiff." It must obtain the court's leave to file a complaint against a third party more than 14 days after serving its original answer.
    - (2) The third-party defendant:
        * (A) Must assert rule 12 defenses.
        * (B) Must assert 13(a) counterclaims, may assert 13(b) counterclaims, and may assert 13(g) crossclaims against other third-party defendants.
        * (C) May assert any of the third-party plaintiff's defenses against the primary plaintiff.
        * (D) May assert claims [counterclaims?] against the primary plaintiff arising from the same subject matter as the plaintiff's claim against the third-party plaintiff.

---

[72]Casebook p. 749.

- (3) Primary plaintiff may assert claims against third-party defendant arising from the same subject matter as the plaintiff's claims against the third-party plaintiff. The third-party defendant must assert rule 12 defenses and rule 13(a) counterclaims, and may assert rule 13(b) counterclaims and rule 13(g) crossclaims.
- (4) Any party may move to strike, sever, or try separately the third-party claim.
- (5) Third-party defendants can assert this rule against any nonparty.
- (6) [Admiralty/maritime jurisdictions]

- (b) When a plaintiff may bring in a third party: same rules as for defending parties.

7.11 *Banks v. City of Emeryville*

7.12 FRCP 24: Intervention

1. (a) Intervention of right.
2. (b) Permissive intervention.
3. (c) Notice and pleading required.

§ 8 Discovery

1. Discovery consists of **(1) interrogatories, (2) requests for production or inspection, and (3) depositions.**[73]

2. Fuller disclosure leads to the most favorable case for each party.[74]

3. Legitimate purposes: promotes settlement, helps determine whether a case can be decided in a summary judgment.

4. Less legitimate purposes: inflict costs, harass, "reconstruction" (i.e., put into the record facts that aren't true).

5. State discovery rules generally track the federal rules.

6. The discovery process:

    (a) *Informal investigation*: happens outside the compulsory structure of formal discovery—interviews, document review, property visits.

    (b) *Discovery plan*: FRCP 26(f) requires parties to agree to a discovery plan.

    (c) *Initial disclosures*: mandatory disclosures include (1) names and contact details of relevant individuals, (2) copies or descriptions of records, (3) computations of damages, and (4) insurance information. FRCP 26(a)(1)(A). Parties are only required to disclose information that is favorable to their cases.[75]

    (d) *Depositions*:

    　　i. Depositions are binding but expensive. Lawyers generally depose all unfriendly witnesses.[76]

    　　ii. FRCP 30 defines the scope of depositions.

    　　iii. Lawyers can instruct defendants not to answer to (1) preserve a privilege, (2) enforce a protect order limiting discovery, or (3) stop abusive behavior.

    (e) *Interrogatories*: written questions that must be answered under oath, often with accompanying requests for documents. FRCP 33 governs interrogatories.

    (f) *Production*: items can be obtained by subpoena if necessary. FRCP 34 controls.

    　　i. **Privileges**: privileged information is not subject to discovery. Common law privileged relationships include attorney-client, spouse-spouse, doctor-patient, clergy-penitent, and others that vary by state.

---

[73] Casebook p. 9.
[74] Casebook p. 882.
[75] Casebook p. 885.
[76] Casebook p. 886.

ii. **Work product**: an attorney's work product is privileged. *Hickman*. See **Work-Product Doctrine** below.

(g) *Physical and mental examinations*: only when physical or mental states are issues in the case. FRCP 35 controls.

(h) *Requests for admission*: to determine whether facts are accurate and documents genuine. FRCP 36.

(i) *Motions for protective orders and motions to compel*: court must award attorneys' fees to the winning party. FRCP 26(c), 37(a)(1).

(j) *Sanctions*: most commonly an award of costs.

8.1 FRCP 26: Duty to Disclose; General Provisions Governing Discovery

- (a) Required disclosures.
    - (1) Initial disclosure.
        * (A) Generally:
            · (i) Names and contact details.
            · (ii) Copies or descriptions of documents, etc.
            · (iii) Computation of damages.
            · (iv) Insurance details.
        * (E) Parties must supplement disclosures when required under 26(e).
- (b) Discovery scope and limits.
    - (1) Parties can discover all nonprivileged matter relevant to claims or defenses. It need not be admissible at trial if it is *reasonably calculated* lead to the discovery of admissible evidence.
    - (2) Limitations on frequency and extent.
        * (A) Court can alter limits.
        * (B) Electronic information need not be produced if it carries undue burden or cost.
        * (C) Court must limit discovery under certain circumstances (enumerated within).
    - (3) Trial preparation: materials [i.e., work product—see *Hickman*].
        * (A) Tangible things prepared for litigation are not discoverable, unless:
            · (i) They are discoverable under 26(b)(1).
            · (ii) There is substantial need or they cannot be obtained without undue hardship.
        * (B) Mental impressions, etc. are excluded [i.e., only facts are discoverable].

8 DISCOVERY

- * (C) People can access their own statements.
- (c) With good cause, the court can protect material from discovery.
- (d) After the initial discovery meeting under 26(f), discovery can proceed in any sequence.
- (e) Supplements and corrections are sometimes required.
- (f) Conference of the parties; planning for discovery.
    - (1) Parties must confer as soon as practicable.
    - (2) Parties must submit a discovery plan within 14 days.
    - (3) Requirements for the discovery plan.

8.2 FRCP 29: Stipulations about Discovery Procedure

8.3 FRCP 30: Depositions by Oral Examination

- (a) When a deposition may be taken.
- (b) Notice of the deposition; other formal requirements.
    - (1) Notice.
    - (2) Producing documents.
    - (6) Notice or subpoena directed to an organization.
- (c) Examination and cross-examination; record of the examination; written questions.
    - (1) Conducted as they would be at trial.
- (d) Duration; sanction; motion to terminate or limit.
    - Limited to one day of seven hours.

8.4 FRCP 33–36

- 33: Interrogatories to Parties.
- 34: Producing Documents, Electronically Stored Information, and Tangible Things, or Entering onto Land, for Inspection and Other Purposes.
- 35: Physical and mental examinations.
- 36: Requests for admission.

8.5 Privileges and Sanctions

1. There were several privileged relationships under the common law, including attorney-client, spouse-spouse, doctor-patient, clergy-penitent, and others that vary by state. There is also the Fifth Amendment privilege against self-incrimination.

2. Privileged information is not discoverable even if it is relevant to the litigation.

3. Privilege protects the source, not the information itself.

4. Privilege can be waived, even unintentionally.

8.5.1 Work Product Privilege: *Hickman v. Taylor*

The attorney's **work product** is privileged. Work product includes unsworn witness statements, internal memoranda, and the attorney's mental impressions.

1. Enabling broad discovery vs. encouraging adversarial hearings.

2. "Work product" is material prepared in anticipation of trial.

3. Facts:

    (a) February 7, 1943: tug J.M. Taylor sank; five of nine crew drowned.

    (b) March 4, 1943: public hearing at United States Steamboat Inspectors where the four survivors testified.

    (c) March 29, 1943: Fortenbaugh privately interviewed survivors and took signed statements. (He conducted other interviews, too, and in some cases made memoranda.)

    (d) November 26, 1943: estate of the fifth dead crew member (here, petitioner) brought suit against the two tug owners and the railroad.

4. Petitioner requested via interrogatories copies of all incident-related records, including signed witness statements, unwritten oral statements, and Fortenbaugh's own memoranda. The court in the Eastern District of Pennsylvania held that the materials were not privileged and ordered disclosure. When the respondents refused, the court held them in contempt. (The contempt order allowed Fortenbaugh to appeal immediately, rather than wait for the trial to end.)

    (a) Under 26(b)(1) alone, these materials would have been discoverable, and they were not protected by attorney-client privilege.

5. The Third Circuit reversed, holding that the requested information was privileged because it was part of the **"work product of the lawyer."**[77]

---
[77] Casebook p. 919.

8 DISCOVERY

6. Justice Murphy:

    - Discovery has two purposes: (1) narrow and clarify the issues in the case and (2) ascertain the facts.
    - The specific rule in question here is irrelevant; what matters is the question of whether "materials collected by an adverse party's counsel in the court of preparation for possible litigation" are privileged.[78]
    - Hickman (petitioner) argued that the privilege to withhold material must be limited to the attorney-client privilege.
    - The attorney-client privilege is not an appropriate framework to answer the question in this case because that privilege does not cover witness interviews or subsequent memoranda, etc.
    - Here, Hickman has requested information that he could have discovered for himself (e.g., testimony of known witnesses). Hickman has failed to show that disclosure of these materials is necessary or that nondisclosure would lead to injustice.
    - The Supreme Court was generally enthusiastic of the liberal FRCP disclosure regime, which was still new at the time.[79] Requiring disclosure of an attorney's work product would lead to "[i]nefficiency, unfairness, and sharp practices."[80] Other arguments against disclosure (in Bradt's framing):
        (a) It would create a disincentive to create the work product in the first place, which might make for worse lawyering.
        (b) "Sweat of the brow" argument: it would be unfair to let an attorney freeride on an opposing attorney's work.
        (c) Mental impressions are inherently private.
    - Affirmed.

7. Justice Jackson, concurring:

    - Restricting discovery preserves adversarial proceedings.
    - Requiring lawyers to disclose their work product would force them to become witnesses for "other witnesses' stories."[81]

8. Parts of *Hickman* codified in FRCP 26(b)(3):

    (a) The definition of work product and its broad protection.
    (b) "But a common law trial is and always should be an adversary proceeding. Discovery was hardly intended to enable a learned profession to perform its functions either without wits or on wits borrowed from the adversary."[82]

---

[78] Casebook p. 920.
[79] Casebook p. 920.
[80] Casebook p. 923.
[81] Casebook p. 925–926.
[82] Casebook p. 925.

8 DISCOVERY

(c) Work product immunity is limited when there is "substantial need" or the threat of "undue hardship."

8.5.2 Work-Product Doctrine

1. In 1970, the FRCP were amended to include an exception for work-product materials in 26(b)(3): material "prepared in anticipation of litigation or for trial . . . "

2. The work-product doctrine can be overcome only if the information cannot be obtained or can only be obtained with great difficulty.[83]

3. Courts (including the *Hinckman* court) are divided on whether attorneys must disclose unrecorded recollections of witnesses' statements.

4. Work product is only protected if it was prepared specifically for the possibility of litigation (though the specific case may not matter).

5. Witnesses must still be disclosed before trial.

6. Discovery sanctions:

    (a) FRCP 26(g): courts must sanction violations of the 26(g) certification requirement.

    (b) FRCP 30: failure to attend a deposition or to subpoena a witness for a deposition is sanctionable.

    (c) FRCP 37: (1) If a court orders disclosure, it must award costs to the winning party. (2) If a party disobeys a judicial order, the court must order it to pay expenses.

    (d) The severity of sanctions are left to district courts.[84]

8.5.3 FRCP 37: Failure to Make Disclosures or to Cooperate in Discovery; Sanctions.

- (a) Motion for an order compelling disclosure or discovery.

    – (1) Must include a showing of a good faith attempt at discovery or obtaining disclosure without court action.

- (b) Failure to comply with a court order.

---

[83] Casebook p. 929.
[84] Casebook p. 977.

§ 9 Summary Judgment

1. **12(b)(6) motion for dismissal for failure to state a claim**: tests the **sufficiency of the allegations themselves.** Assuming the plaintiff's allegations are true, the court determines whether there is a cause of action. State equivalent is the demurrer. Motions to dismiss are based on the pleadings themselves; any additional factual allegations will cause the motion to be treated as a motion for summary judgment.

2. **Rule 56 motion for summary judgment**: tests the **sufficiency of the *facts supporting* the allegations.** Either side can challenge the legal sufficiency of the other's factual allegations or legal contentions.

    (a) Granted if the judge determines that "there is not genuine dispute as to any material fact and the movant is entitled to judgment as a matter of law." Rule 56(a).

    (b) Exists to decide issues that are so one-sided that a trial would be wasteful.[85]

    (c) Pleadings do not support motions for summary judgment[86]—i.e., the motions for summary judgment must be supported with facts, not allegations.

    (d) "...one of the prime uses of discovery is to gather information that will be useful in supporting and opposing summary judgment."[87]

    (e) **Burden of production**: plaintiff must produce sufficient evidence on each element of the case for a jury to reasonably rule in its favor. Otherwise, under FRCP 50, the judge may grant judgment as a matter of law.[88]

    (f) **Burden of persuasion**: the standard by which a plaintiff will have to convince a jury (which, in civil cases, is "by a preponderance").[89]

    (g) Summary judgment tests the whether a party can meet the burden of production.

    (h) **The moving party must support its motion for summary judgment.** If the moving party could successfully move without showing reason to believe that the other party will not be able to meet the burden of production, the motion for summary judgment would be a discovery device.

---

[85] Casebook p. 992 n. 1.
[86] Casebook p. 993 n. 2
[87] Casebook p. 993.
[88] Casebook p. 994–95 n. 4.
[89] Casebook p. 994 n. 4

ID: 9 SUMMARY JUDGMENT

9.1 FRCP 56

- (a) Court can grant summary judgment if "there is not genuine dispute as to any material fact and the movant is entitled to judgment as a matter of law."

- (b) Parties may file motions within 30 days after the close of discovery.

- (c) Procedures.
    - (1) Supporting factual assertions.
    - (2) Facts must be admissible.
    - (3) Court can consider materials not cited in the motion.
    - (4) Affidavits/declarations.

- (d) When facts are unavailable to the non-movant.

- (e) Failing to properly support or address a fact.

- (f) Judgment independent of the motion. [Courts can grant summary judgments absent motions from any party.]

- (g) Failing to grant the requested relief. [If the summary judgment doesn't end the case, its outcome can still come into play during trial.]

- (h) Court can impose sanctions for bad faith affidavits/declarations.

9.2 Summary Judgment: *Adickes v. S.H. Kress & Co.*

To win a motion for summary judgment, **the moving party must show an absence of any genuine issue of fact** when the evidence is viewed in the light most favorable to the opposing party.

1. Sandra Adickes, a white teacher, took a group of black students to Kress restaurant in Hattiesburg, Mississippi. She was refused service and then arrested for vagrancy.

2. She alleged that (1) she was refused service because she was part of a mixed-race group and (2) the refusal of service and subsequent arrest resulted from a conspiracy between Kress and the Hattiesburg police. The District Court for the Southern District of New York directed a verdict for the defendants on the first count and granted summary judgment on the second. The Second Circuit unanimously affirmed.

3. The Supreme Court reversed on both counts (but the edited opinion in the casebook addresses only the summary judgment on the second count).

4. Justice Harlan:

9 SUMMARY JUDGMENT

(a) To show conspiracy as alleged, Adickes must show (1) that an employee of Kress deprived her of her constitutional rights and (2) that the defendant acted "under color of law" (which is satisfied if an employee and the policeman "somehow reached an understanding to deny Miss Adickes service"[90]).

(b) Summary judgment was inappropriate because the respondent, Kress, "failed to carry its burden of showing the absence of any genuine issue of fact"[91] (and any material it submitted "must be viewed in the light most favorable to the opposing party"[92]).

(c) In this case, the two big factual gaps were that the police officers failed to "foreclose the possibility" that they (1) were in the store and (2) influenced the Kress employee to not serve Adickes.[93]

(d) Because respondent did not meet the burden of establishing the police officers' presence, petitioner was not required to file opposing affidavits.

(e) Reversed.

9.3 Celotex Corp. v. Catrett

The movant for summary judgment bears the initial burden of production, i.e., he must clearly show that there is no factual dispute. If the responding party will bear the burden of persuasion at trial, the moving party need only show that the record contains no evidence that the nonmovant will be able to prove an essential element of its case.

More simply: the defendant can successfully claim that plaintiff's case is unfounded if there is no evidence in the record at that time that the plaintiff can make its case.

1. Catrett died in 1979. In 1980, his wife (respondent) filed suit against 15 asbestos companies, including Celotex (petitioner).

2. Celotex moved for summary judgment for lack of evidence showing that its product was a proximate cause of Catrett's death, including a lack of witnesses who could testify to that effect. Catrett produced three documents she claimed demonstrated "a genuine material factual dispute."[94] Celotex argued that the documents were inadmissible hearsay.

3. The District Court for D.C. granted the motions from Celotex and the other defendants. Catrett appealed only the grant for Celotex. The D.C. Circuit reversed on the grounds that Celotex failed to show any evidence to support its motion.[95]

---

[90]Casebook p. 986.
[91]Casebook p. 987.
[92]Casebook p. 988.
[93]Casebook p. 990.
[94]Casebook p. 996–97.
[95]Casebook p. 997.

4. Justice Rehnquist:

    (a) The D.C. Circuit's opinion was inconsistent with FRCP 56. The plaintiff bears the burden of proof for its claim, and in this case the defendant's motion contended that the plaintiff failed to establish the existence of an element essential to its case.

    (b) The moving party need not negate its opponent's claim.

    (c) "One of the principle purposes of the summary judgment rule is to isolate and dispose of factually unsupported claims or defenses, and we think it should be interpreted in a way that allows it to accomplish this purpose."[96]

    (d) Reversed.

9.4 *Arnstein v. Porter*

[Copyright infringement suit against Cole Porter. We skipped it in class.]

9.5 Disagreement about the Existence of a Dispute of Material Fact: *Scott v. Harris*

Courts sometimes disagree about whether there is a genuine dispute of material fact. Courts have broad discretion to evaluate whether a dispute exists.

1. Harris fled from the police in a high-speed car chase. Deputy Scott bumped Harris's car during the chase, causing him to crash and become quadriplegic.

2. Harris sued in district court for violation of the Fourth Amendment. The legal question was whether a police officer can "take actions that place a fleeing motorist at risk of serious injury or death in order to stop the motorist's flight from endangering the lives of innocent bystanders."[97]

3. Scott filed a motion for summary judgment based on qualified immunity. The district court denied, holding that there were significant disagreements about issues of fact which required submission to a jury.

4. The Eleventh Circuit affirmed.

5. Justice Scalia:

    (a) The standard for reviewing motions for summary judgment is to view the evidence in the light most favorable to the nonmoving party.

    (b) Here, however, a videotape "quite clearly contradicts the version of the story told by respondents."[98]

---

[96] Casebook p. 998.
[97] Casebook p. 1015.
[98] Casebook p. 1017.

(c) Eight Supreme Court justices believed the video obviously showed that Harris posed an imminent threat. Therefore, Scott obviously had a qualified immunity to use deadly force and his summary judgment motion should have been granted.

(d) Reversed.

6. Justice Stevens: the video shows that Harris was *not* endangering others. In any case, the district court and the appellate court are more familiar with the local roads.

§ 10 Jury Trials

1. **Burden of production**: a party's duty to produce enough evidence to have the issues decided by a factfinder. Failing to meet the burden of production can result in judgment as a matter of law.

2. **Burden of persuasion**: a party's duty to convince the factfinder—e.g., the plaintiff's duty to show a preponderance of the evidence in favor of his claim.

3. Pre-verdict motions:

4. **Judgment as a matter of law** (directed verdict). FRCP 50. Granted if there is "but one conclusion that reasonable men could have reached." *Simblest*.

5. Post-verdict motions:

6. **Renewed judgment as a matter of law** (judgment n.o.v). FRCP 50. Same standard as pre-verdict JMOL. Must have been raised and denied before the jury's verdict.

7. **New trial**: Granted because of weak evidence or procedural errors. Courts should not grant new trials unless the verdict is against the "great weight" of the evidence. *Spurlin*. Rule 59 controls.

8. **Conditional ruling**.

9. **Altering or amending a judgment**

10.1 Overview and Background

1. Very few cases go to trial.[99]

2. As of 2002, 2/3rds of federal trials were heard before a jury, while 97% of all state trials were heard before a judge.[100]

3. Pre–jury verdict motions: nonsuit, directed verdict (state) or judgment as a matter of law (federal).

4. Post–jury verdict motions: judgment n.o.v. (state), judgment as a matter of law (federal), or new trial (both).[101]

5. A party waives the right to a jury trial if it does not request it. FRCP 38.

6. Seventh Amendment guarantee to a jury trial does not apply to the states.[102]

---

[99] Casebook p. 1057.
[100] Casebook p. 1058.
[101] Casebook p. 1060.
[102] Casebook p. 1098.

10 JURY TRIALS

7. Six and twelve are the most common jury sizes. Six is the lower limit.

8. The Supreme Court has upheld non-unanimous verdicts. FRCP 48 requires a unanimous verdict unless the parties stipulate otherwise.

10.2 Judgment as a Matter of Law: *Simblest v. Maynard*

There are three steps in reviewing a motion for judgment as a matter of law:

1. Review all of the evidence in the record.

2. Draw all reasonable inferences in favor of the non-moving party.

3. Avoid making credibility determinations or weighing the evidence.

If there is only one reasonable outcome, the motion can be granted before or after the jury's verdict.

1. A travelling salesman collided with a fire truck in an intersection in Burlington. He claimed that the power went out when he was in the middle of the intersection, including the traffic lights. All other witnesses testified that the power had gone out at least ten minutes before.

2. He looked to his right when he was half or three-fourths of the way through the intersection. That was the first time he saw the fire truck. He claimed to have not heard the siren nor seen the flashing lights.

3. The salesman sued for negligence to recover for injuries he suffered from the collision.

4. At the close of the plaintiff's case, the defendant moved for a directed verdict. Denied.

5. The jury found for the plaintiff. The defendant moved for judgment n.o.v., which the judge granted.

6. The plaintiff argued, first, that the district court granted the judgment n.o.v. in error.

    (a) The court here explained the standard of review for judgments n.o.v. **"that, without weighing the credibility of the witnesses or otherwise considering the weight of the evidence, there can be but one conclusion as to the verdict that reasonable men could have reached."**[103] Evidence must be viewed in the light most favorable to the non-moving party.

---
[103]Casebook p. 1165.

10 JURY TRIALS

(b) A key question is whether the court can consider *all* evidence or only evidence favorable to the non-moving party and all uncontradicted, unimpeached evidence against him. Vermont law would allow all evidence. The plaintiff argued that the federal rules would allow only favorable evidence. The court here held that the federal standard also allows admission of uncontradicted, unimpeached evidence.

(c) Under either rule, however, the court believed it was clear that the plaintiff was guilty of contributory negligence. Thus, the judgment n.o.v. for the defendant was properly granted.

7. The plaintiff argued in the alternative that the district court erred in declining to instruct the jury on last clear chance. The court dispatched with this argument with the conclusion that "the overwhelming, uncontroverted evidence demonstrates that defendant in the exercise of due care simply could not have avoided the accident."[104]

8. The *Simblest* court developed a three-part test for determining whether a jury could reasonably find for the non-moving party:[105]

    (a) Review all of the evidence in the record.

    (b) Draw all reasonable inferences in favor of the non-moving party.

    (c) Avoid making credibility determinations or weighing the evidence.

9. Courts rarely grant pre-verdict motions for judgment as a matter of law, because if the case is successfully appealed, it will have to be retried entirely from the beginning. However, if the judge grants a motion for judgment after a matter of law after the jury has returned a verdict, a successful appeal will only reinstate that jury's verdict.

10.3 Reasonable Inference of Negligence: *Sioux City & Pac R.R. Co. v. Stout*

If a judge thinks the facts could give rise to a reasonable finding in favor of the non-moving party, the judge can decide to deny the motion for judgment as a matter of law.

1. A six-year-old was injured while playing on an unlocked railyard turntable. His parents brought an action for negligence. The jury returned a verdict of $7,500 for the plaintiff.

2. The court reasoned that if the evidence led to a reasonable inference of negligence, it was free to find for the plaintiff. In this case, because it was reasonable to think that an unlocked turntable might lead to injuries for kids playing on it, negligence was a reasonable inference.

---

[104]Casebook 1169.
[105]Casebook p. 1170 n. 2.

10 JURY TRIALS 87

3. "... although the facts are undisputed it is for the jury and not for the judge to determine whether proper care was given, and whether they establish negligence."[106]

4. What distinguishes this case from *Simblest*? The facts are disputed in both. In both, the court held in substance that the facts were in dispute. In *Simblest*, however, the judge did not believe that the facts could give rise to a reasonable finding in favor of the plaintiff. In this case, however, the judge believed it was reasonable to infer the defendant's negligence.

10.4 FRCP 50: Judgment as a Matter of Law in a Jury Trial; Related Motion for a New Trial; Conditional Ruling

- (a) Judgment as as matter of law.
- (b) Renewing the motion after trial; alternative motion for a new trial.
- (c) Granting the renewed motion; conditional ruling on a motion for a new trial.
- (d) Time for a losing party's new-trial motion.
- (e) Denying the motion for judgment as a matter of law; reversal on appeal.

10.5 FRCP 59: New Trial; Altering or Amending a Judgment

1. (a) In general.
2. (b) Time to file a motion for a new trial.
3. (c) Time to serve affidavits.
4. (d) New trial on the court's initiative or for reasons not in the motion.
5. (e) Motion to alter or amend a judgment.

10.6 Overview of Post-Trial Motions

1. A court can do two things after a jury returns a verdict:[107]

    (a) Enter judgment against the verdict-winner—i.e., judgment as a matter of law (federal law) or judgment n.o.v. (state).

    (b) Grant a new trial because of weak evidence or procedural errors.

---
[106]Casebook p. 1175.
[107]Casebook p. 1180.

10.7 Sacredness of Juries: *Tanner v. United States*

Activity within the jury room is given extraordinary privilege.

1. Petitioners Conover and Tanner were convicted of conspiring to defraud the United States. The Eleventh Circuit affirmed.

2. The petitioners argued that the district court erred in refusing to admit juror testimony at a post-verdict hearing on juror intoxication during the trial.

3. Evidence shows that multiple jurors were drinking, smoking marijuana, and taking cocaine throughout the trial. One of the jurors involved reported the activity to the petitioner's attorney. The district court denied motions for leave to interview jurors or for an evidentiary hearing.

4. Justice O'Connor:

    (a) The firm common law rule is that juror testimony cannot impeach a jury verdict. A few exceptions exist for "external" influence, e.g., when a juror had applied for a job in the D.A.'s office. Juror testimony is not allowed on "internal" influences, including allegations of insanity or lack of understanding of English.

    (b) The rule exists to protect jurors from harassment and to preserve the jury's independence.

    (c) "There is little doubt that post-verdict investigation into juror misconduct would in some instances lead to the invalidation of verdicts reached after irresponsible or improper juror behavior. It is not at all clear, however, that the jury system could survive such efforts to perfect it."[108]

    (d) The legislative history of the Federal Rules of Evidence suggest that Congress explicitly rejected a version of the rules "that would have allowed jurors to testify on juror conduct during deliberations, including juror intoxication."

    (e) Petitioners argue that the refusal to hold an evidentiary hearing at which jurors could testify violates the Sixth Amendment guarantee to a competent jury. The court held that nonjuror evidence and the inadmissibility of juror testimony rendered a post-verdict evidentiary hearing unnecessary.

5. Justice Marshall, dissenting:

    (a) The Federal Rules of Evidence (here, 606(b)) does not preclude juror testimony on conduct before or after deliberations. Because the allegations of misconduct here involved juror activity beyond deliberation, it should have been admitted.

---
[108] Casebook p. 1184.

10 JURY TRIALS

(b) Justice Marshall has a different reading of the legislative history.

(c) Regarding the internal/external influence distinction, as "a common sense matter, drugs and alcohol *are* outside influences on jury members.

10.8 New Trials: *Spurlin v. Gen. Motors*

Courts should not grant new trials unless the verdict is against the "great weight" of the evidence.

1. A school bus crashed in Alabama when its brakes failed. Several suits against General Motors were consolidated. The jury awarded $70,000 in each wrongful death case. The court granted General Motors's motions for judgment n.o.v. and, in the alternative, a new trial on the grounds that the evidence did not support the verdict.

2. On the judgment n.o.v.:

    (a) The *Boeing v. Shipman* standard for reviewing judgments n.o.v. is that the court should consider *all* evidence in light of all reasonable inferences favorable to the party opposed to the motion. If there is substantial evidence opposed to the motion, it must be denied.[109]

    (b) In this case, witness testimony established substantial evidence that the braking system on the bus was not reasonably safe and thus that GM had breached its duty as a manufacturer.

    (c) Judgment n.o.v. reversed.

3. On the motion in the alternative for new trial:

    (a) Seventh Amendment guarantees strong protections for jury verdicts.

    (b) District Courts should not grant motions for new trials unless the jury verdict is at least "against the *great* weight of the evidence."[110]

    (c) The evidence in this case was "at best conflicting." In such cases, courts are not free to set aside jury verdicts.

    (d) Grant of new trial overturned.

---

[109] Casebook p. 1191.
[110] Casebook p. 1195.

§ 11 Appeals

1. The right to appellate review exists when (1) the court violated procedure or (2) the court's decision rested on "misapplication of the substantive law or gross misapprehension of the facts."[111]

2. **Final judgment rule**: appeal is generally allowed only from final judgment, though interlocutory appeal is allowed under some circumstances. 28 U.S.C. § 1291. For instance, FRCP 23(f) allows interlocutory appeal of class certification decisions.[112]

    (a) The **collateral order exception** allows appeal of decisions that don't end the litigation but must "nonetheless be treated as final." *Digital Equip. Corp.*

3. Scope of appeal:

    (a) Appellants must **preserve the issue**—i.e., questions on appeal generally **must have been raised during trial**.

    (b) On **questions of fact**, appellate courts give great deference to trial courts. The standard of review for bench trials is **"clearly erroneous"**. Rule 52(a)(6). The standard of review for jury trials is **complete absence of proof** (because of the re-examination clause in the Seventh Amendment).

    (c) Appellate do not give deference in **pure questions of law**. The standard of review is **de novo**.

    (d) Appellate courts will not overrule decisions within the "sound discretion" of the trial judge unless abuse of discretion is apparent.

    (e) Harmless or nonprejudicial errors will not be reversed. 28 U.S.C. § 2111.

    (f) Appellate courts do not accept new evidence.

    (g) Appellant must specify matters on appeal.

    (h) The scope of injunctive relief is generally limited to abuse of discretion.

    (i) Excessive or inadequate verdicts are appealable (Gasperini).

4. State courts often hear mooted cases to decide important questions of law. Federal courts observe stricter standards on mooted cases because of Article III's cases and controversies restriction.

5. The Supreme Court can review state cases that rely on federal issues. 28 U.S.C. § 1291.

6. Parties that have intervened in litigation have a right to appeal.

---
[111] Casebook p. 1325.
[112] Casebook p. 1326.

11 APPEALS 91

11.1 Collateral Order Doctrine: *Digital Equip. Corp. v. Desktop Direct*

The collateral order exception allows appeal of decisions that don't end the litigation but must "nonetheless be treated as final."

1. Desktop sued Digital for use of the "Desktop Direct" name. The two reached a confidential settlement which included a waiver of all damages and dismissal of the suit. Desktop filed a notice of dismissal in district court.

2. Months later, Desktop discovered that Digital had misrepresented material facts during settlement negotiations. It moved to vacate the dismissal. The court vacated the dismissal and Digital appealed.

3. The Tenth Circuit dismissed the appeal for lack of jurisdiction under 28 U.S.C. § 1291, holding that the district court's order to vacate the dismissal neither ended the litigation nor fell within the "collateral order exception.

4. Justice Souter:

    (a) The **collateral order doctrine** allows appeal from "a narrow class of decisions that do not terminate the litigation, but must . . . nonetheless be treated as 'final.'"[113]

    (b) Digital argued that its "right not to stand trial" under its private settlement agreement required the protection of immediate appeal. It argued that its right was analogous to the qualified immunity right in *Mitchell*.

    (c) The Supreme Court held that the right Digital asserted can be adequately protected once final judgment had been rendered at trial. If it allowed Digital's interlocutory appeal, other types of decision would also be subject to interlocutory appeal—including claims of lack of personal jurisdiction, that the statute of limitations has run, that no material fact is in dispute, and others.[114]

    (d) " . . . such a right by agreement does not rise to the level of importance needed for recognition under § 1291."[115]

    (e) Affirmed.

11.2 28 U.S.C. § 1257: Supreme Court Review of State Court Decisions

- (a) The Supreme Court can review decisions from state courts of last resort.

---

[113] Casebook p. 1347.
[114] Casebook p. 1349.
[115] Casebook p. 1350.

11.3 28 U.S.C. § 1291: Federal Appellate Court Jurisdiction

Federal appellate courts can hear appeals "from all final decisions of the district courts of the United States . . . "

11.4 28 U.S.C. § 1292: Federal Interlocutory Appeals

- (a)(1) Federal appellate can hear appeals from interlocutory orders from district courts.

- (b) Appellate courts can decide whether an order from a district court "involves a controlling question of law as to which there is a substantial ground for for difference of opinion and that an immediate appeal from the order may materially advance the ultimate termination of the litigation . . . "

§ 12 Preclusion

1. **Res judicata** (claim preclusion): a claim (and related claims) cannot be relitigated after final judgment.[116] Requirements:

   (a) Same parties as A1.

   (b) Final judgment on the merits (yes: judgment after trial affirmed on appeal; no: PJ, SMJ, venue; gray area: 12(b)(6), SJ, failure to prosecute, dismissal under sanction—which count as adjudications on the merits in federal court [41(b)]).

   (c) Same cause of action as A1 (same transaction or occurrence).

   (d) Narrow exceptions: agreement/statute, egregious judgment in A1, lack of jurisdiction over A1 (*Staats*).

   (e) Applies only to the **same claimant**. We want plaintiffs to bring all of their claims at once.

2. **Collateral estoppel** (issue preclusion): an issue of fact or law cannot be relitigated after final judgment. Requirements:

   (a) Same issue.

   (b) Actually litigated and decided.

   (c) Full and fair opportunity to litigate.

   (d) Necessary to the judgment.

   (e) Applies **only to parties in the original suit** (*Taylor*).

3. **Claim preclusion bars claims that were never raised. Issue preclusion requires that they were fully litigated.**

4. **Mutuality**: collateral estoppel only applied to the same parties in A1. No longer the case after *Bernhard*.

5. **Taylor**: no virtual representation. You cannot be precluded from arguing an issue if you were not a party in A1.

6. **Defensive non-mutual collateral estoppel**: shield. A defendant can prevent a plaintiff from relitigating a claim that he had previously asserted and lost against another defendant (*Blonder-Tongue*). Gives plaintiffs the incentive to join all potential defendants in the first action.

7. **Offensive non-mutual collateral estoppel**: sword. A plaintiff seeks to prevent a defendant from relitigating an issue the defendant had lost in an earlier trial. May be unfair because the defendant may not have had an incentive to vigorously litigate the issue in the earlier case. It encourages a "wait-and-see" strategy on plaintiffs' part. The court has discretion to disallow preclusion if (1) the plaintiff could have easily joined A1 and (2) it's not somehow unfair to the defendant. *Parklane*.

---

[116] Casebook p. 1224.

12 PRECLUSION 94

8. When filing a claim, failing to file a related claim can prevent the claimant from litigating that claim in the future.

9. Some states define "claim" more narrowly–e.g., California relies on the "primary right," allowing two suits based on the same facts to be brought separately if they are based on the same primary right.[117]

10. Restatement (Second) of Judgments, § 24(2): "What factual grouping constitutes a 'transaction,' and what groupings constitute a 'series,' are to be determined pragmatically, giving weight to such considerations as whether the facts are related in time, space, origin, or motivation, whether they form a convenient trial unit, and whether their treatment as a unit conforms to the parties' expectations or business understanding or usage."[118]

11. Failure to assert a compulsory counterclaim generally bars that claim from future actions.[119]

12. Intervenors must pursue their claims or be barred by claim preclusion in future actions.[120]

13. Res judicata generally applies to causes of action but not to parties.[121]

14. A claim is precluded if a court has entered final judgment on the merits. The definitive final judgment is a trial verdict affirmed on appeal. **Non-final judgments** include dismissals for problems with subject matter jurisdiction, personal jurisdiction, or venue. Most other types of judgment (failure to state a claim, summary judgment, dismissal for failure to follow court orders) generally count as final. The question is whether the plaintiff had an opportunity to be heard on the merits.

15. Parties have an incentive to settle to avoid preclusion, though this gives a significant bargaining advantage to the first plaintiff.

12.1 Consequences of Final Judgment: *Federated Department Stores, Inc. v. Moitie*

Once a claim reaches final judgment, parties cannot raise other claims arising from the same transaction or occurrence. Res judicata overrides competing policy concerns. It is usually worth keeping a case alive on appeal.

1. The government brought an antitrust suit against Federated Department Stores and others. Seven plaintiffs filed civil actions, including Moitie

---
[117] Casebook p. 1238.
[118] Casebook p. 1239.
[119] Casebook p. 1240.
[120] Casebook p. 1240.
[121] Casebook p. 1241.

12 PRECLUSION

in state court (*Moitie I*) and Brown in the Northern District of California (*Brown I*). The civil claims followed the govenment's claims almost verbatim, although Moitie referred only to state law.

2. *Moitie I* was removed to district court. All civil claims were directed to the same federal judge.

3. The district court rejected all of the civil claims for failure to allege an "injury" to their "business or property" under § 4 of the Clayton Act.[122]

4. Five of the plaintiffs appelaed in the Ninth Circuit. The lawyer representing Moitie and Brown, however, chose to refile in state court (*Moitie II* and *Brown II*).

5. *Moitie II* and *Brown II* were removed to federal court. The court found that they were "in many respects identical" to the earlier claims. It dismissed them under res judicata.[123]

6. While *Moitie II* and *Brown II* were pending appeal, the Supreme Court decided *Reiter v. Sonatone Corp.*, holding that retailers *could* allege an "injury" to their "business or property" under § 4 of the Clayton Act, and accordingly the Ninth Circuit reversed the five cases pending appeal. The Ninth Circuit also reversed the dismissals of *Moitie II* and *Brown II* on the same grounds, even though it violated a strict interpretation of res judicata, becuase "the doctrine of res judicata must give way to 'public policy' and 'simple justice.'"[124]

7. Justice Rehnquist:
   (a) "...such an unwarranted departure from res judicata is unwarranted. Indeed, the decision below is all but foreclosed by our prior case law."[125]
   (b) "The doctrine of res judicata serves vital public interests beyond any individual judge's determination of the equities in a particular case."[126]
   (c) Reversed.

8. Justice Blackmun, concurring:
   (a) There may be cases where policy concerns override res judicata.
   (b) *Brown II* should not even been allowed in federal court because *Brown I* was res judicata.

9. Justice Brennan, dissenting:
   (a) Agree with Blackmun that *Brown I* was res judicata.

---

[122] 15 U.S.C. § 15.
[123] Casebook p. 1225.
[124] Casebook p. 1226.
[125] Casebook p. 1227.
[126] Casebook p. 1229.

12.2 Claim Preclusion: *Davis v. DART*

A plaintiff must bring all causes of action related to the same claim. Any related actions he fails to bring are barred from future suits. Preclusion is harsh.

1. 2001: Davis and Johnson alleged race discrimination and retaliation under Title VII and violations of the First and Fourteenth Amendments under 42 U.S.C. § 1983 against Dallas Area Rapid Transit and its Chief of Police. They originally brought the claim in state court and it was removed to Texas district court (*Davis I*). The district court dismissed the claims with prejudice.

2. 2002: Davis and Johnson brought another action in district court alleging similar (but not identical) claims. The court granted summary judgment for the defendants on the grounds that (1) they failed to raise an issue of fact about whether their nonselection for promotion was racially motivated and (2) res judicata from *Davis I* precluded the remaining claims.

3. The Fifth Circuit identified four factors for barring claims under res judicata:

    (a) Identical parties.
    (b) Prior judgment from a court of competent jurisdiction.
    (c) Prior judmgent that was final and on the merits.
    (d) Same cause of action in both suits.

4. Only the fourth factor was disputed here. The standard of review for the Fifth Circuit was (1) whether the barred claims were part of the same cause of action ("same nucleus of operative facts") and (2) whether Davis and Johnson could have advances the barred claims in *Davis I*.[127]

5. The court here found that the claims in both cases "originate from the same continuing course of allegedly discriminatory conduct" and that the claims could have been brought together (despite the plaintiff's argument that their pending EEOC claim prevented bringing the full action in court).

12.3 Claim Splitting: *Staats v. County of Sawyer*

If the initial forum lacks jurisdiction to adjudicate the entirety of the plaintiff's claims, the remaining claims are not barred from future litigation.

1. The county eliminated Staats' job. He believed the county based its decision on disability discrimination. He filed a state law claim with the Wisconsin Equal Rights Division, which authorized a hearing before an administrative judge. That judge found for Staats. On appeal, the Labor

---
[127]Casebook p. 1233.

12 PRECLUSION

and Industry Review Commission rejected his claim and the state court affirmed.

2. Meanwhile, he filed charges with federal Equal Employment Opportunity Commission, which issued him a right-to-sue letter. The district court rejected his federal claims on the ground of claim preclusion.

3. The Seventh Circuit here held that the initial state forum did not have jurisdiction to hear the entirety of Staats' claim. Rather, the circumstances required **claim splitting** between that forum and another. "...Staats had no way to consolidate his WFEA, ADA, and Rehabilitation Act claims in any single forum. He was forced to split his claims and litigate them in separate fora."[128] Staats was not precluded from bringing his federal claims in another forum.

4. Reversed.

12.4 Collateral Estoppel: *Levy v. Kosher Overseers Ass'n of Am.*

To have preclusive effect on issues, the final judgment on the merits must have evaluated an identical issue.

1. KOA applied to the PTO to register a mark containing a K within a circle. Levy (d.b.a. OK Labs) filed an "opposition" with the PTO's Trademark Trial and Appeal Board. The TTAB sustained the opposition and refused KOA's application.

2. KOA did not appeal the TTAB's decision. It kept using the mark.

3. OK sued in federal court. The court granted summary judgment against KOA on the collateral estoppel effect of the TTAB's decision and granted a permanent injunction.

4. The Second Circuit held that there are four factors to apply collateral estoppel to bar litigation:[129]

    (a) Identical issues.

    (b) Prior proceeding "must have been actually litigated and actually decided.

    (c) Full and fair opportunity for litigation in the prior proceeding.

    (d) Final judgment on the merits.

---

[128]Casebook p. 1246.
[129]Casebook p. 1252.

5. The court agreed with KOA's argument that the TTAB applied a different test than a federal court would (under the Lanham Act) in evaluating the claims of "likelihood of confusion." The TTAB did not consider actual usage of the mark, whereas a federal court would apply the "Polaroid factors."[130]

6. Reversed.

12.5 Informal Proceedings and Issue Preclusion: *Jacobs v. CBS*

To have an issue-preclusive effect, the earlier proceeding must have had adequate procedural safeguards.

1. Givens wrote a manuscript for a TV show. He contracted with Westwind to pitch the show to CBS. Under the "First Agreement," CBS agreed to acquire the broadcast rights. Under the "Second Agreement," CBS bought all rights and agreed to credit Webb and Jacobs as Executive Producers.

2. CBS later produced a show based on a similar premise. It did not credit Givens. The Writers' Guild of America concluded that Givens was not a "participating writer" and refused to represent him in arbitration against CBS.

3. Meanwhile, Givens, Jacobs, Webb, and Westwind sued CBS in California state court. CBS removed to federal court and Givens dropped out.

4. CBS moved for summary judgment, arguing that the plaintiffs' claims were completely derivative of Givens' claim and that the WGA's determination that Givens was not a participating writer had a collateral estoppel effect. The court granted the motion.

5. The plaintiffs argued that the WGA proceedings could not have an issue-preclusive effect because they lacked adequate procedural safeguards.[131] The Ninth Circuit agreed. Reversed.

12.6 Virtual Representation: *Taylor v. Sturgell*

1. Herrick, an airplane enthusiast, unsuccessfully sued the FAA for disclosure of documents under FOIA.

2. Taylor, a fellow aviator, sued for disclosure of the same documents. The D.C. Circuit held that Taylor's claim was precluded because Herrick was Taylor's "virtual representative." The Tenth Circuit affirmed.

---

[130] Casebook p. 1253.
[131] Casebook pp. 1259–1260.

12 PRECLUSION 99

3. The Supreme Court reversed, holding that "one is not bound by a judgment in personam in a litigation in which he is not designated as a party or to which he has not been made a party by service of process."[132]

12.6.1 Preclusion Against Other Parties: *Parklane Hosiery v. Shore*

1. **Mutuality rule**: before 1940 or so, collateral estoppel only applied to mutual parties—i.e., one party should not be bound unless the opposing party would have been bound if the judgment had gone the other way.[133]

2. In *Bernhard v. Bank of America*, the California Supreme Court developed a three-part rule for applying collateral estoppel to absent parties:[134]

    (a) Are the issues identical?

    (b) Was there a final judgment on the merits?

    (c) Was the party against whom the collateral estoppel plea is pleaded a party or in privity with a party to the prior judgment?

3. Shore brought a stockholders' class action in district court against Parkland, alleging false and misleading statements about a merger.

4. Earlier, the SEC had brought "essentially" the same claims against Parklane, winning in district court and in the Second Circuit.[135]

5. Shore moved for partial summary judgment on the ground that Parklane was collaterally estopped from relitigating the same issues that had been resolved in its suit against the SEC. The district court denied and the Second Circuit reversed.

6. Justice Stewart:

    (a) There are two key questions on appeal: does collateral estoppel preclude relitigating facts resolved adversely in an earlier hearing? And would such preclusion violate the Seventh Amendment's guarantee of a trial by jury?

    (b) On the first question (preclusive effect of issues decided in an earlier hearing):

        i. *Defensive* collateral estoppel: a plaintiff cannot assert a claim that he had previously litigated and lost against another defendant. (See *Blonder-Tongue Laboratories, Inc. v. Univ. of Ill. Found.*, where the Court held that a patentee could not relitigate the validity of a patent after it had already been held invalid.)[136]

---

[132]See Bradt handout, 11/19/12.
[133]Casebook p. 1279.
[134]Casebook p. 1280.
[135]Casebook p. 1281 top.
[136]Casebook pp. 1282–1283.

12 PRECLUSION

- ii. *Offensive* collateral estoppel: a plaintiff seeks to prevent a defendant from relitigating an issue resolved against it in a prior hearing.[137]
- iii. Defensive collateral estoppel gives plaintiffs an incentive to join all potential defendants in the first action, while offensive collateral estoppel creates the opposite incentive.
- iv. Offensive collateral estoppel may be unfair in some cases because defendants may not have had the incentive to vigorously litigate the issue in the earlier hearing.
- v. Offensive collateral estoppel was allowable in this case.

(c) On the second question (Seventh Amendment):

- i. Rulings in equity have been held to have preclusive effect without violating the Seventh Amendment.[138]
- ii. Parklane argued that the scope of the Seventh Amendment should be determined with reference to the common law in 1791, which allowed collateral estoppel only when there was mutuality of parties.
- iii. Subsequent development have refined the scope of the jury's function. "...these developments are not repugnant to the Seventh Amendment simply for the reason that they did not exist in 1791."[139]
- iv. Collateral estoppel applied. Affirmed.

7. Justice Rehnquist, dissenting:

(a) Deprivation of trial by jury was one of the key grievances in the American Revolution.

(b) "...to sanction creation of procedural devices which limit the province of the jury to a greater degree than permitted at common law in 1791 is in direct contravention of the Seventh Amendment."[140]

---

[137] Casebook p. 1283.
[138] Casebook p. 1287.
[139] Casebook p. 1288.
[140] Casebook p. 1291.

§ 13 Class Actions

1. Class actions can involve either plaintiff classes (common) or defendant classes (rare).

2. Binding determinations can be made upon class members who are absent, unnamed, and sometimes unnotified.

3. "... in almost all class actions the attorney's financial investment, ideological stake in the outcome, and potential to influence the conduct of the case is much greater than that of the named class representative."[141]

13.1 FRCP 23: Class Actions

1. Rule 23 was revised in 1966 with three goals in mind:[142]

    (a) Define cases where the benefits of a class suit outweigh the disadvantages.

    (b) Specify that all class suits are binding and define the scope of their preclusive effect.

    (c) Ensure maximum advantage and fair representation for absent class members.

2. The rule's specific provisions are:

    - (a) Requirements applicable to all class actions.
        - (1) **Numerosity**: the class must be so numerous that joinder is impracticable.
        - (2) **Commonality**: there must be questions of law or fact common to the class (a "not particularly stringent requirement"[143]).
        - (3) **Typicality**: the claims or defenses of the representative party must be typical of those of the class as a whole.
        - (4) **Fair and adequate protection of the interests of the class**: the named parties must represent the entire class's interest—e.g., it must avoid conflicts of interest, and the class must not include groups with "sharply differing interests."footnoteCasebook p. 799. The representation by the class attorney must also be adequate.
    - (b) Types of class actions.
        - (1) Class treatment is allowed when (A) individual suits would result in incompatible standards of conduct for the non-class or (B) individual suits would impair the ability of those who have

---
[141]Casebook p. 799 n. 1.d.
[142]Casebook p. 797.
[143]Casebook p. 798 n. 1.b.

13 CLASS ACTIONS 102

   not brought individual suits, e.g., in "limited fund" suits where the fund is insufficient to adequately cover the number of possible individual claims. Generally limited to suits seeking injunctive or declaratory relief.

   – (2) Class treatment is allowed when the party opposing the class has "acted or refused to act on grounds that apply generally to the class." Civil rights suits are the most common.

   – (3) Class treatment is allowed when questions common to the class "predominate" over questions affecting individual class members, and class action must be "superior" to other methods of adjudication. Notice to class members is mandatory and members must have the option of opting out of the class (unlike (b)(1) and (2) actions).

13.2 *Chandler v. Southwest Jeep-Eagle, Inc.*

To establish class certification, a plaintiff must meet all four requirements of 23(a) and all of the requirements of one of the three subsections of 23(b).

1. Chandler sued Southwest Jeep-Eagle over "misrepresentations and unfair and deceptive practices in connection with Southwest's standard retail installment contract." Chandler sought class certification on two counts.[144]

2. The court reasoned that to establish class certification, Chandler must pass a two-part test. First, he must meet all requirements of 23(a). Second, he must meet one of the requirements of 23(b)—in this case, 23(b)(3).

3. The court found that Chandler's claims met all four elements of 23(a)—numerosity, commonality, typicality, and adequacy of representation.[145] It also held that Chandler met both elements of 23(b)—a predominating common question of law or fact and a showing that a class action is superior to other methods of litigation.[146]

4. The court granted Chandler's motion for class certification.

13.3 *Wal Mart Stores, Inc. v. Dukes*

1. Female employees of Wal Mart brought a Title VII action seeking injunctive and declaratory relief, back pay, and punitive damages.

2. The district court granted class certification under 23(b). The Ninth Circuit substantially affirmed.

3. Justice Scalia:

---
[144] Casebook p. 814.
[145] Casebook pp. 816–19.
[146] Casebook pp. 819–21.

(a) Class certification was inconsistent with 23(a) because only a corporate policy could implement the widespread discrimination that would satisfy the rule's requirement of a common question of law or fact, and no such policy existed.

(b) Class certification was inconsistent with 23(b)(2) because the rule prevents monetary relief that is not incidental to the injuntive or declaratory relief. Claims for back pay must be evaluated individually. To hold otherwise would abridge Wal Mart's substantive rights.

www.ingramcontent.com/pod-product-compliance
Lightning Source LLC
Chambersburg PA
CBHW062221220526
45471CB00009B/3292